Jew and Gentile Reconciled:
An Exploration of the Northern Tribes in Pauline Literature

JEW AND GENTILE RECONCILED:
AN EXPLORATION OF THE NORTHERN TRIBES IN PAULINE LITERATURE

Bryan E. Lewis

GlossaHouse
Wilmore, KY

Jew and Gentile Reconciled:
An Exploration of the Northern Tribes in Pauline Literature

© GlossaHouse, LLC, 2016

All rights reserved. No part of this book may be reproduced or transmitted in any form or by any means, electronic or mechanical, including photocopying or recording, or by means of any information storage or retrieval system, except as may be expressly permitted by the 1976 Copyright Act or in writing from the publisher. Requests for permission should be addressed in writing to the following:

GlossaHouse, LLC
110 Callis Circle
Wilmore, KY 40309
www.GlossaHouse.com

Jew and Gentile Reconciled:
An Exploration of the Northern Tribes in Pauline Literature
Lewis, Bryan E. – Wilmore, KY: GlossaHouse, © 2016.

v, 173 cm. — (GlossaHouse thesis series; vol. 1)
A revision of the author's M.A. thesis, Amridge University, 2015
Includes bibliographical references and indices.

ISBN: 9781942697121 (pb)
        9781942697251 (hb)

1. Bible. Romans, IX, 24-26—Criticism, interpretation, etc. 2. Gentiles in the Bible. 3. Outsider in the Bible. 4. Ethnicity in the Bible. 5. Paul, the Apostle, Saint—Views on Gentiles. 6. Reconciliation—Biblical teaching. 7. Bible. Hosea, I, 9-10—Criticism, interpretation, etc. 8. Bible. Hosea, II, 23—Criticism, interpretation, etc. I. Title. II. Series.

BS2665.52.L484 2016   227/.06

Library of Congress Control Number: 2016933175

The fonts used to create this work are available from www.linguistsoftware.com/lgku.htm

Cover design by T. Michael W. Halcomb
Text layout and book design by Carl S. Sweatman & T. Michael W. Halcomb

*To my wife, **Holly:***

*For gracing me
with your love and beauty
these past twenty-two years of marriage.*

*"Many women have done excellently,
but you surpass them all."
(Prov 31:29)*

GLOSSAHOUSE THESIS SERIES

SERIES EDITORS
T. MICHAEL W. HALCOMB
FREDRICK J. LONG
CARL S. SWEATMAN

VOLUME EDITOR
CARL S. SWEATMAN

GLOSSAHOUSE THESIS SERIES

The goal of the GlossaHouse Thesis Series is to facilitate the creation and publication of innovative, affordable, and accessible scholarly resources, whether print or digital, that advance research in the areas of both ancient and modern texts and languages.

Table of Contents

ABBREVIATIONS	i
FIGURES	ii
PREFACE	iii–v
CHAPTER 1 Introduction	1–32
CHAPTER 2 Preliminary Considerations	33–56
CHAPTER 3 The Northern Tribes of Israel	57–76
CHAPTER 4 Return from Exile as a Second-Temple Period Expectation	77–111
CHAPTER 5 Paul's Appropriation of Hosea 1:9–10 and 2:23 in Romans 9:24–26	112–147
CHAPTER 6 Conclusion	148–151
BIBLIOGRAPHY	153–163
INDICIES	164–173

ABBREVIATIONS

The abbreviations used throughout this thesis follow the standard established by the *SBL Handbook of Style* (1999). Those employed that do not appear in the *Handbook* are (listed according to abbreviation):

BBMS	Baker Biblical Monograph Series
BECNT	Baker Exegetical Commentary on the New Testament
BHT	Beitrage zur Historischen Theologie
CPNIV	College Press NIV Commentary
NICNT	New International Commentary on the New Testament
SBJT	*Southern Baptist Journal of Theology*

List of Figures

4.1	Jer 31:34 in Rom 11:27	86
5.1	Exod 32:32 in Rom 9:3	114
5.2	Exod 32:32 in Rom 9:3 (English)	114
5.3	Gen 18:10 and 18:14 in Rom 9:9	122
5.4	Gen 18:10 and 18:14 in Rom 9:9 (English)	122
5.5	Gen 48:19 in Rom 11:25b	126
5.6	Gen 48:19 in Rom 11:25b (English)	126
5.7	Isa 11:10 in Rom 15:12	131
5.8	Isa 11:10 in Rom 15:12 (English)	131
5.9	Isa 29:16 in Rom 9:20b	135
5.10	Isa 29:16 in Rom 9:20b (English)	135
5.11	Hos 8:8 in Rom 9:21	136
5.12	Hos 8:8 in Rom 9:21 (English)	137
5.13	Hos 1:10 and 2:23 in Rom 9:25–26	140
5.14	Hos 1:10 and 2:23 in Rom 9:25–26 (English)	141

Preface

This thesis is primarily concerned with the Apostle Paul's use of Hos 1:9–10 and 2:23 in Rom 9:24–26. The study itself is located against the milieu of well-established literary critical methods. Therefore, in this study, comprehensive attention is given to the original context of Paul's quotations, allusions, and echoes. By employing the hermeneutical methods of detection first set forth by Richard B. Hays, I conduct an examination of Paul's Old Testament context while simultaneously juxtaposing his text against relevant textual traditions.

With this in mind, I posit that there is a "narrative substructure" that lies underneath the text and within Paul's own theological reflection, which provides the proper framework for understanding and interpreting his intentions in Rom 9. I suggest that Paul commonly used Israel's Scripture in harmony with its original intention. Paul likely understood that many of the northern tribes of Israel were not, in fact, completely destroyed by the Assyrians in the eighth century BCE and lost to time, but instead had acculturated with heathen non-Israelites, thereby losing their identity and effectively becoming "not my people," or Gentiles. Thus, Paul understands his call to the Gentiles to be intricately tied to Israel's hope for the end of her exile, and therefore, to be coterminously bringing about its fulfillment through his Gentile mission in the first century CE. Consequently, I argue that Paul's appropriation of Hos 1:9–10 and 2:23 in Rom 9:24–26 is likely employed intentionally to evoke the promise of Israel's restoration as a robust metanarrative in Paul's efforts toward Jewish and Gentile reconciliation.

The writing of this thesis has spanned several major transitions in my family's life; therefore, an immense debt of gratitude first belongs to them. To my wife, my dearest friend and my companion in life, who insisted that I remain in academia at times when I was ready to quit. And, to my children, Brittnee, Kaylee, and Joshua—thank you for sacrificing my absence so this study could become a reality. May you always choose enlightenment over ignorance.

My mother, Sherry I. Swift, likewise deserves some praise. Without her early example—i.e., a single mother struggling through community college—I would have likely never began my academic journey.

My sincere thanks go to the members of my thesis committee, outstanding scholars and long-suffering mentors all: Dr. Daniel Fletcher, Dr. Michael Strickland, and Dr. Paul Watson. Your incisive minds, insatiable inquisitiveness, and intellectual honesty will continue to inspire me as I move forward in my academic journey. Along these lines, I would also like to acknowledge both my colleagues and the staff at Amridge University, Turner School of Theology, who have also supported me in various other ways. Particularly, Dr. Rodney Cloud and Dr. Carl Byrd for always going above and beyond the call on my behalf. Likewise, Dr. Joel S. Williams, who also provided a respectable amount of input into this study. It has been particularly gratifying to be associated with an astonishing group of scholars.

Vanderbilt Divinity Library also deserves a mention: I am grateful for the privilege of being allowed access to your facilities for the purposes of my research. Likewise, thanks to you and the Divinity School for going over and above the call in my years on campus as both an employee and a student.

Thanks are also due to those who interacted with early versions of my thesis: Tim Hall, for his brotherly friendship, discerning criticism, and encouragement throughout the course of this project.

Likewise, Jack Scott, Mickey Denen, Don Preston, and Tami Jelinek, who all read major portions of the manuscript in progress and posed insightful questions that helped to improve my arguments. I cherish the way in which God has knit our hearts and minds together.

Special thanks are also due to the magnificent team at GlossaHouse: Dr. Michael Halcomb, Dr. Fred Long, and Dr. Carl Sweatman for giving me the opportunity to publish this thesis. Particularly, I would like to thank Carl Sweatman for his patience and editorial prowess. Carl you saved me from many abominable errors.

Finally, I am most thankful to God, who is the ultimate provider of all these life's blessings. In the course of my own academic journey, he has seen my voyage of faith through some trying times. Therefore, I offer these words to all. This work is "written so that you may come to believe that Jesus was indeed Israel's Messiah, the Son of God, and that through believing you may have life in his name" (John 20:31).

B.E. Lewis
Nashville, Tennessee
Palm Sunday, 2016

Chapter 1
INTRODUCTION

1.1. "Not My People"

> Including us whom he has called, not from the Jews only but also from the Gentiles? As indeed he says in Hosea,
> "Those who were not my people
> I will call 'my people,'
> and her who was not beloved
> I will call 'beloved.'
> "And in the very place where it was said to them,
> 'you are not my people,'
> there they shall be called
> children of the living God."[1]

Initially the words, "Not my people" (cf. Hos 1:9–10; 2:23 [MT: לֹא־עַמִּי] [LXX: οὐ λαός μου])[2] were part of an indictment by YHWH against the northern tribes of Israel for their violation of the covenant. In a manner evocative of the later sign-acts of both Jeremiah and Ezekiel,[3] Hosea is told to marry a "wife of

---

[1] Rom 9:24–26. All Scripture quotations, unless otherwise indicated, are taken from *The New Oxford Annotated Bible: New Revised Standard Version with the Apocrypha* (Oxford: Oxford University Press, 2010).

[2] For the MT used in this study, see K. Elliger and W. Rudolph, eds., *Biblia Hebraica Stuttgartensia* (Stuttgart: Deutsche Bibelgesellschaft, 1997). For the LXX used in this study, see Alfred Rahlfs and Robert Hanhart, eds., *Septuaginta* (Stuttgart: Deutsche Bibelgesellschaft, 2007).

[3] Sign-acts were types of non-verbalized communication whose purpose was to illustrate the ramifications of impending doom to the observers.

whoredom," who in turn bears children whose names are symbolic apogees of the northern kingdom of Israel's judgment by YHWH as carried out by the Assyrians. As Hosea's narrative unfolds, a son named, יזרעאל "Jezreel" (= "God sows") is born, followed by a daughter named, לארחמה "Lo-Ruhamah" (= "no mercy"), and finally, another son named, לאעמי "Lo-Ammi" (= "not my people"). According to the Hosean writer,[4] religious pluralism—particularly, worship of the Canaanite pantheon,[5] along with

---

However, a number of Hebrew Bible scholars hold that the sign-acts did more than "illustrate" an imminent event; in fact, they initiated the event. The same argument occurs with regard to the Lord's Supper: is it "representational" or is it "sacramental?" Another example would be Ezekiel, who baked bread over human dung and laid on his side—symbolic actions describing the coming siege of and famine in Jerusalem (Ezek 4:9–17). Likewise, Jeremiah was forbidden to marry and have children—a reminder of the imminent threat of Jerusalem's destruction (Jer 16:1–9).

[4] The consensus of biblical scholarship seems to agree with the initial suggestions set forth by Karl Graf, Julius Wellhausen, and Martin Noth. That is, the book of Hosea was filtered through the pen of either an exilic or post-exilic deuteronomistic redactor. With this in mind, I have chosen to use inclusive language that takes into account this possibility. It is not the task of this study to address the question of Hosean authorship. Regardless of authorship, the book is clearly rooted in the life of Israel at the time of the rise and threat of Assyrian power. Moreover, my concern has to do with Paul's use of Hosea; whether or not the Hebrew Bible narrative has succumbed to some sort of evolutionary development is inconsequential. Paul's use of the Hebrew Bible was primarily for theological purposes. That is, by selectively employing parts of history, Paul's motive was to create a "theological narrative," which had immediate significance for his own contemporaries as an exemplary catalyst for eliciting faith in Israel's Messiah. I shall discuss this more in chapter 2.

[5] E.g., Baal and Asherah. The inscription found on the 8th-century BCE *pithoi* at Kuntillet Ajrud, "Yahweh of Samaria and his (A)asherah" provides adequate evidence that the worship of Asherah was fixed within Samaria's socio-religious practices. The most common debate is whether or not this inscription refers to a consort of YHWH. However, this issue is not a useful inquiry for this study. For the inscription see *Pithos* A, in Ze'ev Meshel,

Israel's portentous use of a *machtpolitik* (1 Kgs 21:1–15; 2 Kgs 9–10)—had reached such a zenith, that the Lord ultimately decided to "break the bow of [northern] Israel" (an idiom for military defeat). Punishment would be meted out by initially sowing them among the Gentile nations (Hos 8:8 [MT: בגוים] [LXX: ἐν τοῖς ἔθνεσιν]). Ultimately speaking of the Assyrian deportation and repopulation program, this scattering of the northern kingdom's tribes among the heathen nations is pictured in Hosea as the sowing of seed. However, as we shall see momentarily, this same metaphor is also employed reciprocally to symbolize their ingathering, restoration, reconciliation, and resurrection in the "last days."[6]

Secondly, YHWH performed the northern tribes' rebuke by his decision to no longer show them mercy (Hos 1:6). Third, by issuing a symbolic divorce, the northern kingdom's special standing as the covenant people of YHWH was lost and their status was changed to "not my people" (Hos 1:8). That is, as I shall demonstrate, the northern tribes of Israel would become an eclectic mix of people with no discrete national identity, scattered to the Gentile nations, and thus, outside the covenant community of YHWH—effectively becoming Gentiles (ἔθνη).

1.2. Paul's Appropriation of "Not My People"

Over 700 years later, in his letter to the Romans, the Apostle Paul ostensibly appropriated this phrase in a manner insouciant to

---

Kuntillet 'Ajrud: A Religious Centre from the Time of the Judean Monarchy on the Border of Sinai (Jerusalem: The Israel Museum, 1978).

[6] I share the view of N. T. Wright, R. T. France, et al., that the "last days" are not referring to the end of the space-time continuum, but to the end of the present evil age or present world order (Paul's time). This is in keeping with the Second-Temple Judaic apocalyptic expectation that יהוה (YHWH) would soon break into the world and set the world to rights—e.g., Paul expected the dawning of the age of salvation soon, in contrast to his own age "the present evil age" [τοῦ αἰῶνος τοῦ ἐνεστῶτος πονηροῦ] (Gal 1:4).

its original meaning. Moreover, throughout the history of Christianity, the majority of interpreters have maintained that Paul's quotation of Hos 1:9–10 and 2:23 in Rom 9:25–26 was employed arbitrarily as something completely extraneous to the original significance of the past (I shall demonstrate this claim not to be the case throughout the course of this work). That is, Paul's quotation of Hosea has largely been understood as only applicable to first-century Gentiles, even though, the original meaning was directed to the northern tribes of Israel.[7] Moreover, these Gentiles have been perennially viewed as a detached ethnic group that shares no affinities with the northern tribes of Israel. Unfortunately, these two assumptions have been used historically to provide support to the idea that the Apostle Paul's first-century appropriation of Hos 1:9–10 and 2:23 moved away from its earlier or original meaning in order to make the passage fit with his own later Gentile missional purposes.

For example, in a fourth-century commentary on Paul's letters, Ambrosiaster wrote this about Rom 9:24–26:

> It is clear that this was said about the Gentiles, who once were not God's people, but afterward, to the chagrin of the Jews, received mercy and are called God's people. Once they were not loved, but when the Jews fell away they were adopted as children and are now loved, so that where once they were not called God's people, now they are called children of the living God.[8]

---

[7] By "original meaning" it is meant "original authorial intent." Narrative intertextuality, Jewish hermeneutics, the possibility of multiple meanings, and the question of Paul's possible proof-texting will be discussed in more detail in chapter 2.

[8] Ambrosiaster, *Ambrosiastri Qui Dicitur Commentarius in Epistulas Paulinas* CSEL 81.1 (Vienna: Hoelder-Pichler-Tempsky, 1966), 331—as found

Unfortunately, Ambrosiaster overlooked the original significance to the northern tribes of Israel—applying the quotation to Gentiles only. As a result, he also did not consider a possible distinction between the Israelites and Jews. Likewise, John Chrysostom seemed confident that "Hosea obviously was speaking about the Gentiles here."[9] Like Ambrosiaster, he makes no mention about the possible significance to the northern tribes of Israel.

Theodoret came close to expressing what is in my opinion the full significance of Paul's use of Hos 1:9–10 and 2:23 in Rom 9:24–26:

> This passage originally applied to Jews, not to Gentiles.... It meant that God's people would lose their status and be called "Not my people" and "Not beloved." But then God promised that the rejected Jews would be called back again. Thus from having been God's people and then rejected they would return.... The Gentiles, on the other hand, would become God's people for the first time, having never been his people before.[10]

Unfortunately, Theodoret wrongly equated the "northern tribes of Israel" with the "Jews," thereby making the Jews of Paul's time synonymous with the Israelites in the book of Hosea. Simply put, I disagree with his assertion that the passage "originally applied to Jews." Instead, it originally applied to a distinct group known as the Israelites (i.e., the northern tribes of Israel), who "would lose

---

in Gerald Bray, *Roman,* ed. Thomas C. Oden; ACCS 6 (Downers Grove: IVP Academic, 1998), 266.

[9] John Chrysostom, *Homilies on Romans* (NPNF¹ 11:469)—as found in Bray, *Romans,* 266.

[10] Theodoret of Cyrus, *Interpretation of the Letter to the Romans* (PG 82.43–226).

their status" and then "be called back again" through Paul's Gentile mission. Thus, by saying the northern tribes of Israel became "not my people" and "not beloved," I am saying that they became Gentiles.[11] Conversely, I am positing that their "being called back again" was indeed happening through Paul's first-century Gentile mission. As I shall demonstrate in chapter 2, the term "Jew" did not exist until late in the southern kingdom's Babylonian captivity. Moreover, it is incorrect to suppose that *all* those from the Assyrian conquest *wholly* assimilated into the southern kingdom, so that Israelites and Jews are to be treated as a single homogeneous group. To this, I shall say more in chapter 3.

---

[11] In this study, I do not distinguish between "scattered Israelites" and "Samaritans." I simply use the term "Samaritan" to refer to all the inhabitants of the city and regions of Samaria regardless of their affiliation—or lack thereof—with the Mt. Gerizim community. Regardless of ethnic and religious affiliation, these groups all existed outside of the Jerusalem-centered covenant community of YHWH. That is, whether scattered to the nations or whether they had succumbed to Assyrian populace amalgamation in Samaria, they had undergone a shift in personal identity. This is one reason why, according to Dorothy Lee, the Samaritans were "despised by Jews, treated as Gentiles" ("John," in *New Interpreter's Bible One-Volume Commentary*, eds. David L. Petersen and Beverly R. Gaventa [Nashville: Abingdon, 2010], 710). Nevertheless, it is evident that the Samaritan population—which was once the great capital city of the northern tribes—eventually, became an eclectic mix of people with no discrete Israelite identity. Moreover, while it is possible that the Israelites that remained were allowed to carry on specific cultural practices, or developed them in later generations, the overall thrust of the Assyrian exile and repopulation was on some level also an effort to make the vanquished people groups conform to the ideals and culture of the conquering nation. The *modus operandi* of the Assyrian campaign was to affect a shift in personal identity. This involved forced education into a common language, forced military service, various changes in religious and cultural practices, and especially a forced end to the practice of endogamy. Effectively, this meant becoming Gentile, or, in this case, something other than Israelite. I shall say more on this in chapter 3.

Jean Calvin admitted that Paul's Gentile appropriation was somewhat problematic, yet he still construed Paul's use of Hosea as strictly applying to Gentiles:

> The meaning is clear, but there is some difficulty in the application of the prophecy, for it will not be denied the prophet is referring to the Israelites in that passage. Offended by their crimes, the Lord declares that they are no longer His people. He afterwards says in consolation that He will make those whom He does not love His beloved, and those who are not a people His people. Paul endeavours to apply to the Gentiles this prophecy, which is explicitly addressed to the Jews.[12]

The problem with Calvin's construal is that it does not adequately provide an answer for why Paul ostensibly moved away from the original meaning. Equally, Calvin seems to have blindly assumed that Paul saw the Israelites and Gentiles as two disconnected ethnic groups. This is due in large part to the fact that Calvin considered the Israelites and Jews to be a single homogeneous group (e.g., evident by his own words "referring to the Israelites" and "addressed to the Jews"). In this study, I shall argue the opposite.

Calvin's interpretation of Rom 9:24–26, along with its "difficulty" in application, did not find much more clarity within the world of twentieth-century scholarship, as C.E.B. Cranfield opines:

> The original reference of the Hosea verses was to the northern kingdom of Israel: Paul applies them to the

---

[12] Jean Calvin, *The Epistles of Paul the Apostle to the Romans and to the Thessalonians*, Trans. Ross MacKenzie; eds. David W. Torrance (Grand Rapids: Eerdmans, 1960), 213.

Gentiles (cf. 1 Pet 2.10). The ten tribes were indeed thrust out into the dark realm of the heathen, so that there is real justification for regarding them as a type of rejection. But their restoration was promised in Hosea's prophecy, and Paul takes this promise as a proof of God's purpose to include the Gentiles in His salvation. But, in view of the sequel in chapters 10 and 11, it is most unlikely that Paul did not also have in mind the fact that the original reference was to "that other, rejected Israel," the ten lost tribes, and did not see in those lost tribes of Israel not only a type of the Gentiles but also the type of the unbelieving majority of his Jewish contemporaries.[13]

I would certainly agree with Cranfield when he states: "Paul takes this [Hosea's] promise as a proof of God's purpose to include the Gentiles in His salvation."[14] However, I would disagree that Paul saw in the northern tribes of Israel "only a type of the Gentiles." Instead, as I shall demonstrate, Paul understood that the northern tribes of Israel—due to the numerous repercussions of the Assyrian conquest—had lost their identity among the Gentile nations. Therefore, Paul did not view both the Gentiles and the northern tribes of Israel as two distinct unconnected ethnic groups, but instead, as uniformly homogeneous. Equally, Cranfield seems to portray both "Jew" and "rejected Israel" (i.e., the northern tribes) as an indistinguishable group when he says: Paul saw in "the ten lost tribes...the type of the unbelieving majority of his Jewish contemporaries." However, as I shall demonstrate in chapter 2, it is wrong to blend the two into the same melting pot.

---

[13] C. E. B. Cranfield, *A Critical and Exegetical Commentary on the Epistle to the Romans* (2 vols.; ICC (Edinburgh: T&T Clark, 1979), 2:499–500.
[14] Ibid.

Jack Cottrell's exegesis provides the most adequate elucidation of Paul's appropriation of Hosea to-date when he writes:

> The consensus seems to be that the ten "lost" tribes' permanent exile has so intermingled them with the Gentiles that the evangelization of the group will necessarily involve the evangelization of the other.... These Jews had become "not loved" and "not my people" through the judgment of the exile; the Gentiles were "not loved" and "not my people" by nature, so to speak. Thus in the NT age, when the church goes into all the world, the gospel appeal reaches Jew and Gentile alike, and the words of Hosea take on a new and expanded meaning. Hosea's prophecy specifically promises the restoration of the Jews, but because of their scattered status "Paul takes this promise as a proof of God's purpose to include the Gentiles in His salvation."[15]

In my opinion, Cottrell begins by rightly pointing out that the Assyrian exile had so intermingled the northern tribes with the Gentiles that the evangelization of one group also meant the evangelization of the other. I see this point as the most adequate explanation to-date. However, Cottrell unfortunately also makes the same blunder as Cranfield and others, in that he wrongly conflates the Jews of the Second Temple period with Hosea's Israelites (i.e., the northern tribes of Israel), and thus has viewed them as one homogenous group. He makes this clear when he writes: "Hosea's prophecy was originally addressed to Jews, specifically to the ten tribes of the northern kingdom."[16]

---

[15] Jack Cottrell, *Romans*, vol. 2 (CPNIV; Joplin: College Press, 1998), 134–35—quoting Cranfield.

[16] *Ibid*, 134.

It is crucial that I make a distinction here since later in this study the concepts of "end of the exile," "return from exile," and "restoration and ingathering of Israel" will become fundamental to our explanation of why Paul employs Israel's Scripture in Rom 9:24–26 as he does. As I shall demonstrate, the Apostle Paul was emphatically looking for the fulfillment of YHWH's promise that the northern tribes of Israel would also one day return from exile just as the southern tribes (i.e., the Jews) had already done.[17] Thus, it is critical that I employ a corrective nomenclature. That is, Hosea's prophecy was not originally addressed to Jews (i.e., as Cottrell asserts), but instead, to Israelites.

1.3. Supersessionism and Adversus Iudaeos

The origins of such hermeneutical and exegetical struggles—especially as they concern Paul's use of Israel's Scripture—can be traced back to when supersessionist theologies[18] began to enjoy much hegemonistic success. The tendency has been to construe Paul's theology in a manner that views the church as the complete replacement of a "wicked" Israel. This understanding has led many to make unwarranted distinctions between Israel and the church, and also, by extension, between the northern tribes of Israel and the Gentiles. In fact, this kind of construal has seriously subjugated Paul's concern for the Lord's faithfulness to Israel's promises (Rom 15:8).

For example, Augustine contributed to supersessionism's burgeoning effect when he said, "For in the Jewish people was

---

[17] By saying the southern tribes had returned to the land, I do not mean "all" southern exiles. Such exactitude is not necessary for understanding the historical narrative of the writer. In fact, only a minority of the descendants of the original southern exiles actually returned to Judah. Most remained in Babylon; and of course, some—including apparently Jeremiah—had gone to Egypt.

[18] Supersessionism is essentially the view that the Christian church has replaced Israel. It is sometimes called Replacement Theology.

figured the Christian people."¹⁹ Likewise, in his *Contra Faustum Manichaeum* (340 CE), he compared the Jews with the murder of Cain: "Abel, the younger brother, is killed by the elder brother; Christ, the head of the younger people, is killed by the elder people of the Jews. Abel dies in the field; Christ dies on Calvary...only when a Jew comes over to Christ, he is no longer Cain."²⁰ It is widely understood that Augustine provided an exemplar for much subsequent Christian theology. Since his theological era, his supersessionist views have been exemplified in copious volumes of Protestant Christian contemplation. For example, concerning Augustine's influence upon Protestant theology, Justo González has said:

> Augustine is the end of one era as well as the beginning of another. He is the last of the ancient Christian writers, and the forerunner of medieval theology. The main currents of ancient theology converged in him, and from him flow the rivers, not only of medieval scholasticism, but also of sixteenth-century Protestant theology.²¹

Certainly, John Chrysostom, in his eight sermons (387 CE), demonstrated a whole new level of early Christian anti-Jewish rhetoric. Among other things, he called the Jews "degenerates"²²

---

[19] Augustine, *On the Gospel of John* 11.8 (NPNF¹ 7:77).

[20] Augustine, *St. Augustine's Writings Against the Manichaeans and Against the Donatists,* ed. Richard Stothert (Altenmünster: Jazzybee Verlag, 2012), 186–88.

[21] Justo L. González, *A History of Christian Thought,* 2 Vols. (Nashville: Abingdon, 1987), 2:15.

[22] John Chrysostom, "Sixth Homily Against the Jews," in *Saint John Chrysostom: Discourses Against Judaizing Christians*, eds. Paul W. Harkins and Hermigild Dressler (Washington, DC: Catholic University of America Press, 1999), 68.

proclaiming that their misfortunes were due to God's "absolute rejection of you [Jews]...I hate the Jews."[23] It has been the presence of this anti-Jewish bias within Christian theology that has caused some of the hermeneutical and exegetical struggles that Pauline scholarship is still trying to sort out today.

Finally, influenced by these early church fathers, Martin Luther wrote, "They [the Jews] insist that they are God's people and the church, [but they] are the devil's whore."[24] Among other things, Luther was perturbed at then recent Jewish efforts to convert Christians, so much so that in the course of his verbal bellicosity he did not abstain from advocating violence. Speaking of the Jews, he said:

> In honor of our Lord and of Christendom...set fire to their synagogues or schools...I advise that their houses also be razed and destroyed...all their prayer books and Talmudic writings, in which such idolatry, lies, cursing, and blasphemy are taught, be taken from them...their Rabbis be forbidden to teach henceforth on pain of loss of life and limb...that safe-conduct on the highways be abolished completely for the Jews.[25]

My point here is not to paint Luther (or John Chrysostom and Augustine for that matter) as an anti-Semite. However, much of his rhetoric certainly possessed an anti-Jewish prejudice that aided and abetted a Christian theology, which came to routinely advance an overly excessive amount of dissimilarity between Israel and the

---

[23] *Ibid.*

[24] Martin Luther, *On the Jews and Their Lies* (trans. Martin H. Bertram; Philadelphia: Harpagon, 2014), 625 (Kindle edition).

[25] *Ibid.*, 2007–09.

church.²⁶ Moreover, even though post-Holocaust biblical scholarship has undergone a metamorphosis in thinking and now largely denounces such blatant anti-Jewish writings, the influence of such writings has not yet been completely exorcized from Christian theology.

Adversus Iudaeos writings from the Patristic Period to the Reformation are replete with "new identity" or "replacement" motifs, which repeatedly draw a sharp distinction between Israel and the church. Therefore, much of the blame falls upon the Early Church Fathers, followed by the Reformers, for initially setting Christianity on its theological anti-Jewish course. The result has been the creation of a false dichotomy between Israel and the Church that has since enjoyed a long dominance in Christian theology. Moreover, because of this natural inclination to exegetically pillory the Jews from the text (and the northern tribes of Israel), the ultimate consequence has been to construe Paul's Gentiles as only a non-Israelite truncated group.

Let me state clearly—as I shall show on the basis of the evidence presented in this study—one result of these early Christian anti-Jewish writings has been an improper understanding of the term ἔθνη ("Gentile") and all that it encompasses. Unfortunately, the diachronic development of the term within Christian history has led to a meaning that is strictly non-Israelite.²⁷ However, as I shall demonstrate, it is a term that both expresses and is inclusive of the ultimate restoration and ingathering of the

---

²⁶ For a more thorough examination of Luther's quote, see T. Michael W. Halcomb, *Entering the Fray: A Primer on New Testament Issues for the Church and the Academy* (Eugene, OR: Wipf and Stock, 2012), 178–82.

²⁷ See the section on "terminology" in chapter 2. In that section, I clarify the distinctions between: Gentile, Israelite, and Jew. Though terminological exactitude is hard to obtain, I point out that the terms "Israel" or "Israelite" are not always synonymous with "ethnic Jews" or those exiles that returned from Babylon.

northern tribes of Israel. Subsequently, it is inclusive of the ultimate restoration all humanity—not at some time in the future, as some would have it, but in the past (i.e., in the first century through Paul's Gentile mission).

1.4. Historic and Dispensational Premillennialism

As I have shown, "new identity" or "replacement" motifs undoubtedly existed within the exegetical work of the early church. Unfortunately, they have since increased under various forms of premillennialism.

"Dispensational Premillennialism" was a late nineteen-century development, which ultimately became prevalent in the twentieth century within many evangelical circles. It is John Nelson Darby (1800–1882) who is usually credited as the first to systematize the essential features of this theology. Its sharpest difference from that of its predecessor, "Historic Premillennialism," is that it makes an "absolute distinction between Israel and the church as two separate peoples of God."[28] For example, Lewis S. Chafer, an impenitent proponent of Dispensational Premillennialism, posited a sharp dissimilarity between Israel and the church when he wrote: "God is pursuing two distinct purposes: one related to…Judaism; while the other is related to…Christianity." [29] But not all premillennial advocates have suggested such a clear distinction or separation. For example, George E. Ladd, an influential proponent of Historic Premillennialism, argued for slight continuity between Israel and the church when he wrote: "The church, consisting of both Jews

---

[28] John F. Walvoord, as quoted in Anthony A. Hoekema, *The Bible and the Future* (Grand Rapids: Eerdmans, 1979), 186.

[29] Lewis Sperry Chafer, *Dispensationalism* (Dallas: Dallas Seminary Press, 1936), 107.

and Gentiles, has become the people of God."[30] As we shall see, this view is closely analogous to that of Covenant Theologians.

Nevertheless, we can broadly contend that Dispensational Premillennialism has largely been an evolving theology. As such it is difficult to give a precise definition with specificity. However, for the purposes of this study, the most notable feature is that the distinction often made between Israel and the church has created a nullifying interpretation of Israel's promises, which have ostensibly been momentarily postponed. That is, since the Messiah's offer of the kingdom was "rejected by the Jews, Christ now proceeded to establish the church. The purpose of the church is [now] to gather believers, primarily Gentiles, but inclusive of Jews, as the body of Christ."[31]

As we can see, this particular scheme posits that the church has replaced Israel for a time—i.e., the church is a "parenthesis" or even an "afterthought" in God's original plan.[32] Unfortunately, this particular construal has occasionally served to accentuate the anti-Jewish themes of the early Church Fathers, i.e., God's acceptance of the Gentiles over and against his rejection—temporary or not—of Israel. By advancing an unqualified distinction between Israel and the church, Dispensational Premillennialists have only bolstered "new identity" or "replacement" motifs, thereby once again creating a false dichotomy between Israel and the church.

Additionally, Dispensational schemes posit that all of Israel's restoration promises are to be fulfilled to a "modern," "ethnic," and "national" Israel sometime in the near future. However, I submit that it is a bit anachronistic to make the Apostle Paul's first-

---

[30] George Eldon Ladd, "Historic Premillennialism," in *The Meaning of the Millennium: Four Views*, ed. Robert G. Clouse (Downers Grove: InterVarsity, 1977), 20–24.

[31] Hoekema, *Bible and the Future*, 189.

[32] *Ibid.*

century Israel representative of the "modern state of Israel," as this seriously attacks the authorial intent and historical context of the author. Instead, as I shall demonstrate, these restoration promises were actually accomplished in the past. That is, concerning Israel, there is not a "new" or "separate" set of promises waiting to be fulfilled beyond the "church age." Instead, these promises were indeed realized in the first century. Israel's "being called back again" or their "ingathering" was happening through Paul's first-century Gentile mission. Paul was well aware that all Israel's restoration promises encompassed *the return of both houses of Israel*. By Paul's time, representatives from the southern tribes had returned to the land from exile, but the northern tribes had not. Unfortunately, then, Dispensational Premillennialists are also guilty of equating the northern tribes of Israel with ethnic Jews (Rom 9–11)—and modern Jews at that. That is, Dispensational Premillennialists avoid the fact that Israel's Scripture speaks of two separate exiles.

In this study, I shall argue against such a scheme. I posit that Paul's mission to the Gentiles was actually inclusive of the ingathering of the northern tribes of Israel. Therefore, the gathering of Gentiles and the gathering of Israel are not independent events but coterminous. Both the Old Testament and Second-Temple Jewish literature bear witness to the expectation that in the "latter days" the Gentile nations would be converted to the worship of the YHWH, and as a result, they would flow unto Jerusalem. However, what dispensational schemes often miss is that this expectation is also concerned with the scattered northern tribes of Israel. As I shall show, the expectation of Israel's ingathering into the land was closely tied to the eschatological ingathering of the Gentiles. That is, the messianic gathering of the "holy people" was to be concurrent with the ingathering of "Gentile nations serving him [YHWH] under his yoke" (Isa 2:2–4; *Pss. Sol.* 17:26, 30).

Thus, to separate and push Israel's promises into the future is unjustifiable and must be rejected on the basis that it denies the fact that the Lord kept his promises to Israel *when he said he would*. Moreover, this scheme creates a discontinuity in the narrative unity of redemptive history.

Finally, in the light of the juxtaposition of Dispensational Premillennialism with Historic Premillennialism, a comment about the latter is in order. Simply put, I find no justification for making Israel's promises the "absolute" possession of the church. Like Dispensational Premillennialism, Historic Premillennialism also makes an unqualified distinction between Israel and the church by encouraging a replacement motif. For example, Ladd writes: "The prophecies of Hosea are fulfilled in the Christian church. If this is a 'spiritualizing hermeneutic,' so be it…it is clearly what the New Testament does to the Old Testament prophecies."[33] By saying this, Ladd has argued that Paul abandoned Hosea's original authorial intent for the northern tribes of Israel and appropriated the text with a "new" meaning and "new" significance intended *only* for the Christian church. In other words, Ladd seems to argue that the church has wholly replaced all Israel as the people of God, and thus, the promises became the sole custody of the church. However, this too creates a superfluous distinction between Israel and the church, which was most likely foreign to Paul. As I shall demonstrate in this study, the church was not a distinctive entity from Israel. Instead, Israel was the ἐκκλησία (= "church") in the wilderness (Acts 8:38). Therefore, Israel and the church are actually a homogenous entity.

It is important to note that first-century Christianity was initially Jewish. That is, the first-century ἐκκλησία viewed itself as a part of Israel (i.e., specifically reforming Judaism) and not distinct. In reality, such terms as "Christian" or distinctions such as

---

[33] Ladd, "Historic Premillennialism," 20–24.

a "non-Jewish church," would not have been included in the terminology of a first-century follower of Jesus. Such divisions only began to occur as Supersessionism came to a place of prominence within early Christianity.

1.5. Covenant Theology

Covenant Theology is that branch of Reformed theology that has its roots in "Federal Theology."[34] It seeks to explain how God's redemptive purposes are being worked out for mankind. That is, unlike Dispensational schemes, which seek to divide redemptive-history into a number of distinct "dispensations," Covenant Theology seeks to "organize the history of the world into terms of covenants."[35] Thus, it is usually further broken down into three specific foci, which are played out in this specific order: (1) a covenant of redemption (i.e., a pre-terrestrial agreement between the persons of the Godhead); (2) a covenant of works (i.e., made with Adam—a representative for all of humanity—before the fall); and (3) a covenant of grace (i.e., now made through Christ to all who believe).

Whereas Dispensational schemes see the church as a "new," "replacement," or distinct entity from that old covenant with Israel, Covenant Theology rightly posits that there is more continuity in the Lord's plan with regard to Israel by insisting that God has only

---

[34] Torrance defines it this way: "Federal Theology is that form of theology that gave central place to the concept of covenant and that distinguished different covenants in God's relation to the world" (James B. Torrance, "Covenant or Contract? A Study of the Theological Background of Worship in Seventeenth-Century Scotland," in *Beyond Old and New Perspectives on Paul: Reflections on the Work of Douglas Campbell*, ed. Chris Tilling (Eugene, OR: Wipf and Stock, 2014], 263).

[35] Peter J. Gentry and Stephen J. Wellum, *Kingdom through Covenant: A Biblical-Theological Understanding of the Covenants* (Wheaton: Crossway, 2012), 57.

"one plan of redemption and only one people of God."³⁶ Thus, the restoration promises originally made to Israel are to be understood as fulfilled in the Gentile inclusion into the church. That is, since the first group of Jesus followers was composed of both Jews and Gentiles, Israel's restoration promises were then realized in the church. Thus, the true Israel is now the church and the restoration promises to Israel (particularly the return to the land) only find a spiritual fulfillment within the church.

Unfortunately, I think Covenant Theology's construal is lacking in the same way as Ladd's Historic Premillennialism. Specifically, it does not consider enough of the continuity between the church and Israel. The view that the promises to Israel only find a spiritual fulfillment within the church still makes the church and Israel distinctive entities. Once again, my contention is that Israel was the ἐκκλησία in the wilderness (Acts 8:38), thus making Israel and the church a homogenous entity.

Secondly, Covenant Theology wrongly equates the "northern tribes of Israel" with the "Jews" of the first century. By this I mean, it rightly recognizes that Israel's restoration promises were to be realized in a first-century group of Jesus followers consisting of both Jew and Gentile (i.e., fulfilled in the Gentile inclusion into the church), but then it fails to address the fact that the promises of restoration were made to *both* houses of Israel—i.e., not just to Jews who returned from Babylonian exile, but to Israelites still in Assyrian exile. Thus, either Covenant Theology never addresses the whereabouts of the northern tribes, or it just blindly assumes that they were swallowed up into the southern kingdom at some unknown period of time.

I will demonstrate in this work that the southern kingdom did not necessarily swallow up the northern tribes of Israel. Instead, the latter were either scattered to the Gentile nations or, through

---

³⁶ *Ibid.*

the process of Assyrian populace amalgamation in Samaria, had become one with the Gentiles.[37] Thus, the promises that were made to both houses of Israel (i.e., Israel and Judah) are fulfilled not only in an atemporal sense (i.e., spiritual), but also in a temporal sense (i.e., nonspiritual). That is, though the promises of ingathering were realized in Christ, as advocates of Covenant Theology assert, there was also a literal physical ingathering taking place—as Hosea had foretold (Hos 1:11)—under Paul's mission to the Gentiles.

Even though Covenant Theology rightly seeks to create some continuity between Israel and the church (i.e., Jew and Gentile inclusion), it still renders a reading of Paul that is excessively discontinuous with the full scope of Israel's ingathering and restoration story. I contend that there is room for a better articulation of what Paul is doing with his appropriation in Romans.

1.6. New Covenant Theology

In more recent scholarship, Thomas Schreiner, though an advocate of New Covenant Theology, appears more sympathetic with Covenant Theology by making the usual claim that the church is now the "true Israel" in whom all Israel's promises are fulfilled: "Pauline churches are considered to be the 'true Israel' and 'new temple' of sorts, as they inherited the promises of the chosen nation [Israel]."[38] For Schreiner "the church of Jesus Christ is the 'true' Israel for Paul...it consist of all those Jews or Gentiles who put their faith in Christ."[39] Here we see that Schreiner has followed the traditional Reformed interpretation—one that continues to

---

[37] See note 11 above.

[38] Thomas R. Schreiner, "Paul: A Reformed Reading," in *Four Views on the Apostle Paul*, ed. Michael F. Bird (Grand Rapids: Zondervan, 2012), 12.

[39] *Ibid.*, 41–42.

employ a replacement motif. That is, by advocating such language as "true Israel," "new temple," and the church as the sole inheritor of Israel's promises, Schreiner seems to share an affinity with the idea that Gentile Christianity is the definitive replacement to an inferior Judaism. That is, he seems to encourage the notion that Israel's promises are fulfilled in the church (i.e., a replacement of sorts) and not necessarily a continuance from old covenant times. Again, I posit that Israel and the church are actually homogenous entities.

Likewise, Schreiner seems to endorse this key aspect of Covenant Theology by equating the "northern tribes of Israel" with the "ethnic Jews" of the first century, and then, by conveniently bypassing the fact that the promises of restoration were made to both houses—or *all twelve tribes of Israel*. More specifically, by asserting that the church in the first century consisted of both Jews and Gentiles, Schreiner has failed to account for the plight of the northern tribes of Israel. However, it is crucial to realize that though the Babylonian exile had ended, the Assyrian exile had not.

Douglas Moo seems to leave Schreiner's views behind by offering an alternative reading of Paul's appropriation of Hosea:

> The church is not so much a replacement for Israel or even a "new" Israel; it is the continuation of "Israel" in the era of fulfillment.... Recognizing this continuity in Israel from testament to testament provides a rationale for Paul's application of OT texts about Israel to the Gentiles. Paul can see in Hos 1:10 and Isa 65:1 and Ps 44:22 and Joel 2:32 reference to the Gentiles because Israel, the seed of Abraham, now includes Gentiles. In some sense, what I am proposing is not a lot different than the usual church = Israel construct. But this construct too easily leads to a

complete displacement model that would have Paul uprooting one olive tree and planting another in its place.[40]

While it is extremely encouraging to see Moo avoid various forms of the replacement model, or as he calls it a "displacement model," I think his view does not do enough to move us beyond the Paul's arbitrary hermeneutics debate. That is, I do not think Moo's continuity model fully fleshes out "why" Paul is using Israel's Scriptures to the application and inclusion of Gentiles. As I shall demonstrate, the "rationale for Paul's application of OT texts about Israel to the Gentiles" is more involved than Moo suggests. Paul's construal does indeed posit a "continuation of 'Israel' in the era of fulfillment," but that fulfillment is not only atemporal.

It is hard to be certain as to whether Moo and Schreiner are complete proponents of New Covenant Theology (NCT), but they certainly do seem to be at least somewhat sympathetic with Steve Lehrer's position:

> Then there is the view of NCT, which understands Israel to be an unbelieving type or picture of the true people of God, the church. According to NCT, Israel never was a believing people as a whole. Israel always had a tiny remnant of true believers in her midst. Israel was not the church in the Old Testament, but they did function as a type or picture of the church—the true people of God.[41]

Unfortunately, Lehrer's position is not wholly different from that of traditional Covenant Theology; he reads ancient Israel as a "type

---

[40] Douglas J. Moo, "Paul's Universalizing Hermeneutic in Romans," *SBJT* 11.3 (2007): 77.

[41] Steve Lehrer, *New Covenant Theology: Questions Answered* (Tempe: IDS.org, 2006), 66.

of the antitype—the Christian church."⁴² Lehrer does not see—or at least acknowledge—the full scope of continuity that exists between Israel and the church. That is, Lehrer sees Christ ostensibly bringing about the desuetude of Israel, and thus inaugurating the age of the "new" spiritual church. This reading has two key problems. First, it continues to view Israel and the church as heterogeneous entities. The most startling feature is that despite the plain teaching of Scripture (Acts 8:38), Lehrer maintains, "Israel was not the church in the Old Testament." And second, this reading wrongly equates the "northern tribes of Israel" or "Israelites" with "ethnic Jews." As noted with Schreiner, this bypasses the fact that the *promises of restoration were made to both houses of Israel—or to all twelve tribes of Israel.* For the southern kingdom of Israel (i.e., the Jews), the Babylonian Exile had concluded in 539 BCE. However, the Assyrian Exile had not yet brought a greater portion of Israel (i.e., the northern tribes) back into the land.

Finally, I would agree with the claims of both Covenant Theology and New Covenant Theology that Israel's promises were fulfilled in the work of the Messiah (i.e., Jew and Gentile inclusion). However, I think the use of terms like "new Israel" and "true Israel," and even the employment of "new identity" and "replacement" motifs, create a superfluous narrowing of Paul's more multifaceted concern for Israel's promises—Moo's statement being the exception.

1.7. Status Quaestionis *(Pauline Perspectives Old and New)*

With the state of investigation from the twentieth to the twenty-first centuries came some discontinuity in an anachronistic treatment of Israel's story. This set the stage for some noteworthy advances in the world of Pauline scholarship. Of course, it was

---

⁴² *Ibid.*

Albert Schweitzer who popularized the notion that the best framework for understanding Paul is eschatological.⁴³ Furthermore, scholars such as E.P. Sanders have proposed that Paul's letters must be interpreted through the lens of "Palestinian Judaism."⁴⁴ Certainly, this was a watershed event for Pauline studies, one that seized the attention of Pauline scholarship and turned it toward the obvious nexus between a Jewish Paul and Israel's restoration. This then caused many theologians to judge the dispensational forms of replacement theology as untenable,⁴⁵ thus causing many to share sympathy with what Jewish scholars—especially post-holocaust scholars—have long demurred, the idea that "Judaism must be defective for Christianity to be effective."⁴⁶ Moreover, the serious Pauline scholar cannot discount the hermeneutical revolutionary idea of intertextuality in Paul (to be discussed in the next chapter) and that his theology is informed by Israel's Scriptures (one of the central methods employed in this work).⁴⁷ Furthermore, persuasive arguments have been made that help assuage the anti-Jewishness of the past, by suggesting that the "works of the law did not refer

---

⁴³ Albert Schweitzer, *The Mysticism of Paul the Apostle*, trans. W. Montgomery (New York: Holt and Company, 1931).

⁴⁴ E. P. Sanders, *Paul and Palestinian Judaism: A Comparison of Patterns of Religion* (Philadelphia: Fortress, 1977).

⁴⁵ No one has given more attention to the nexus link between a Jewish Paul and Israel's restoration than N. T. Wright; see *The Climax of the Covenant: Christ and the Law in Pauline Theology* (Edinburgh: T&T Clark, 1992); cf. also *Jesus and the Victory of God* (Minneapolis: Fortress, 1996), 360–61.

⁴⁶ Mark Nanos, *The Mystery of Romans: The Jewish Context of Paul's Letter* (Minneapolis: Fortress, 1996).

⁴⁷ See e.g., Richard B. Hays, *Echoes of Scripture in the Letters of Paul* (New Haven: Yale University Press, 1989); idem, *The Conversion of the Imagination: Paul as Interpreter of Israel's Scripture* (Grand Rapids: Eerdmans, 2005); J. Ross Wagner, *Heralds of the Good News: Isaiah and Paul in Concert in the Letter to the Romans* (Boston: Brill, 2003); Christopher A. Beetham, *Echoes of Scripture in the Letter of Paul to the Colossians* (Leiden: Brill, 2008).

to Jewish legalism, but rather to Covenant Nomism—the idea that Jews did not believe in legalistic works righteousness for salvation, but instead, righteousness is a matter of being a part of God's covenant community."[48] Finally, recent fresh proposals have been offered that seek to get beyond New Perspectives on Paul. Here the arguments hold that there are some interpretative difficulties in Paul's theology first created by the "New Perspective," which has not yet been thoroughly fleshed out.[49]

Though these advances from within biblical scholarship have generated a cacophony of much critical opprobrium from those outside biblio-academia, i.e., among traditional interpreters,[50] they have also proven beneficial in reattaching Paul's theology to Israel's story. This study stands upon their shoulders.

1.8. N.T. Wright, Exile, and the Restoration of Israel

A necessary excursus in this study will involve a discussion of Israel's *two* exiles and the first-century expectation of Israel's restoration, of which more shall be said in chapter four. Some of the most recent and influential works on these themes have come from N.T. Wright.[51] Throughout his key works on the subject, the interrelated themes of late Second-Temple Judaism's restoration

---

[48] James D.G. Dunn, *The New Perspective on Paul* (Grand Rapid: Eerdmans, 2008), 173–92.

[49] Douglas A. Campbell, *The Deliverance of God: An Apocalyptic Rereading of Justification in Paul* (Grand Rapids: Eerdmans, 2009).

[50] E.g., John Piper, *The Future of Justification: A Response to N. T. Wright* (Wheaton: Crossway, 2007).

[51] I have chosen him as my primary dialogue partner because he is fresh on the minds of those both inside and outside of biblical scholarship. Though I could dialogue with other scholars, Wright, with the release of his new book, *Paul and the Faithfulness of God*, seems to be the most relevant to any current discussion on exile in Pauline theology.

hopes and the expectation of the end of the exile are constant motifs.[52]

Here, Wright seems—at least in part—to have built his hypothesis on the work of Sanders who was one of the first to suggest the close interrelatedness of "Jewish monotheism, election, and eschatology,"[53] and among the first to posit that the covenant between God and Israel was central to first-century Judaism. This led to the understanding that exile and restoration are pivotal components for a correct understanding of "Jewish Restoration Eschatology."[54] According to Sanders, first-century Palestinian Jews understood their lack of fidelity towards YHWH's covenant as the cause for suffering the horror of exile. However, along with this condemnation came the promise of future restoration and return from exile, which became a prominent expectation within the Second-Temple period.[55]

Despite the fact that many Jews had long returned to their homeland from the Babylonian captivity, Wright posits that Jews believed their exile to still be in process during the late Second-Temple period. However, it is precisely at this point that Wright makes a superfluous move by suggesting that the Babylonian exile had become an "image" or "metaphor" employed by first-century

---

[52] Wright, *Climax of the Covenant*; idem, *The New Testament and the People of God* (Minneapolis: Fortress, 1992); idem, *Jesus and the Victory of God*; idem *The Resurrection of the Son of God* (Minneapolis: Fortress, 2003); idem, *Paul: In Fresh Perspective* (Minneapolis: Fortress, 2005); idem, *Paul and the Faithfulness of God* (Minneapolis: Fortress, 2013).

[53] Sanders, *Paul and Palestinian Judaism*, 84, 240–69, 511–15. Also, Wright dedicates a chapter to these themes in *Paul: In Fresh Perspectives*, 83-153.

[54] This is Sanders's phrase—see *Jesus and Judaism* (Philadelphia: Fortress, 1985), 77–119, 335; cf. also, *Paul and Palestinian Judaism* 479–511.

[55] Sanders, *Jesus and Judaism*, 77–119.

Jews to refer to their current status under Roman domination.[56] Thus, Wright has reinterpreted exile as a continuing political (and theological) exile rather than simply geographical. In doing this, he has utterly missed the significance of the Assyrian exile.

In a brief excursus, where he examines Wright's "End of the Exile" theme, Brant Pitre[57] offers two helpful points that are worth emphasizing, especially since they will prove foundational to this study.

First, as Pitre points out, "Wright has the right insight, but the wrong exile."[58] The Second-Temple period Jewish hope for the end of the exile was none other than the question, "Where are the northern tribes?" To symbolize or change the meaning away from geographical exile, as Wright attempts to do, "overlooks an absolutely critical fact; there was not only one exile in Israel's history, but two."[59] Though the Babylonian exile had ended, the effects of the Assyrian exile remained. In this way, it was still in progress, but not in the political sense as Wright posits. The northern tribes of Israel still remained scattered or "swallowed up among the Gentile nations [MT: בגוים] [LXX: ἐν τοῖς ἔθνεσιν]" (Hos 8:8)—by now, mostly due to the lingering effects of populace amalgamation. As I shall argue, the population of the northern tribes of Israel had been forced on diverse levels to share in various Gentile national identities. Thus, a loss of both national and personal identity ensued, to which I shall say more in chapter 3.

Nevertheless, the northern tribes of Israel still remained in exile; thus, those Jews in Palestine in the first century would have

---

[56] Wright, *New Testament and the People of God*, 268–69. Wright further explains his position in *Paul and the Faithfulness of God*, 139–41.

[57] See Brant Pitre, *Jesus, the Tribulation, and the End of the Exile: Restoration Eschatology and the Origin of the Atonement*, WUNT 2/204 (Tubingen: Mohr Siebeck, 2005), 31–40.

[58] *Ibid.*, 35.

[59] *Ibid.*, 33.

been both familiar with and expecting the fulfillment of the prophet Hosea's initial promises of restoration. That is: "The *people of Judah and the people of Israel* shall be gathered together, and they shall appoint for themselves one head; and they shall take possession of the land, for great shall be the day of Jezreel" (Hos 1:11—emphasis added). Yet another example can be found in Ezekiel's vision, about which I shall say more momentarily. However, here Ezekiel posited the restoration of *all twelve tribes of Israel*:

> *Thus says the Lord God: I am about to take the* stick of Joseph (which is in the hand of Ephraim) and the tribes of Israel *associated with it; and I will put the* stick of Judah *upon it, and* make them one stick, *in order that they may be* one in my hand. *When the sticks on which you write are in your hand before their eyes, then say to them, thus says the Lord God:* I will take the people of Israel from the nations among which they have gone, and will gather them from every quarter, and bring them to their own land. *I will make them one nation in the land, on the mountains of Israel; and one king shall be king over them all.* Never again shall they be two nations, and never again shall they be divided into two kingdoms. (Ezek 37:19–22—emphasis added)

With regard to Pitre's second point, and this echoes my earlier claim, another point of contention concerning Wright's construal that I share with Pitre is that, like others, Wright equates the Jews of the Second-Temple period with "all Israel" or with "the northern tribes of Israel." That is, he does not seem to make a distinction between Jews and Israelites. However, as I argue in chapter 2, it is a grave error to make the terms "Israelite" and "Jew" identical analogues. More specifically, as I shall show, the northern tribes of

Israel are not synonymous with and did not *fully* assimilate into the Jews (i.e., the southern kingdom) before, during, or after the Babylonian exile.

Finally, though I applaud Pitre for pointing out the significance of two separate exiles, my one quibble is that he never specifically illustrates how the northern tribes returned to the land. His thesis is that the final eschatological tribulation precedes the messianic age of salvation, and thus so does the ingathering, restoration, and end of the exile. Thus, as I will demonstrate, building upon this premise the ingathering of the northern tribes was coterminous with Paul's mission to the Gentiles. In fact, they were one in the same. The Gentile nations—consisting of an eclectic mix of people with no discrete national identity (i.e., the covenantally divorced northern tribes and those who were never part of the commonwealth of Israel)—would be renewed to the worship of YHWH through Paul's mission; and as a result, they would *all* flow unto Jerusalem (i.e., the land [cf. Isa 2:2]).

1.9. Thesis Statement

Despite the fact that Pauline theology has undergone quite the metamorphosis in the last one hundred years, and given the fact that many scholars share in a consensus concerning the prominence of Israel's story in Paul's letters, it is surprising that no detailed monograph exists on Paul's use of Hosea's phrase, "not my people" specifically in Rom 9:24–26. I am only aware of Jason A. Staples's article, "What Do the Gentiles Have to Do with 'All Israel?' A Fresh Look at Romans 11:25–27," [60] which was presented at the Society of Biblical Literature annual meeting in 2008.

---

[60] Jason A. Staples, "What Do the Gentiles Have to Do with 'All Israel?' A Fresh Look at Romans 11:25–27," *JBL* 130.2 (2011): 371–90. Knowledge of Staples's paper came after I began my own research.

In his article, Staples gives the phrase "not my people" only a slight treatment, choosing instead to focus more on the specific meaning of "all Israel" in Rom 11:25–27. Though Staples's article shares many affinities with my own study (e.g., he echoes Paul's concern for the northern tribes of Israel, and also argues for the same reworking of the term "Gentile"), this study attempts to move in a more nuanced direction by explaining how Israel's restoration promises concerning the end of the exile were fulfilled in the first century.

Therefore, the central task of this study is fourfold:

1. It is crucial to determine how Paul appropriates Hos 1:9–10 and 2:23 in Rom 9:25–26. More specifically, we must determine why Paul appropriated Israel's Scripture in a manner that at first glance seems to depart from its immediate historical context or original authorial intent.
2. A more nuanced focus is to determine why Paul applied to Gentiles a message that was initially directed to the northern tribes of Israel. I shall demonstrate that Paul was not simply proof-texting or purposely attempting to change the original meaning of Hosea. Instead, he employed a deliberate hermeneutical scheme to show that the ingathering of the Gentile nations also meant the ingathering of the northern tribes, and conversely, the end of Israel's exile. In Paul's mind, the Assyrian exile had so intermingled the northern tribes with the Gentiles that he understood them to be a single homogenous group.
3. Thus, in this study, I will suggest that Paul was not attempting to appropriate Hosea's message as something anachronistic to his own audience. Instead, he was expressing a dual concern for the still-in-exile northern tribes of Israel, who were not, in fact, completely destroyed

by the Assyrians in the eighth century BCE and thus lost to time, but had acculturated with heathen non-Israelites, thereby losing their identity and effectively becoming "not my people," or Gentiles.

4. Therefore, Paul's first-century ministry to the Gentiles is not unconnected from the northern tribes' story. Instead, it is intimately connected—so much so that Paul understands his call to Gentiles to be intricately tied to Israel's hope for the end of her exile, and therefore, to be simultaneously bringing about its completion through the ingathering of the northern tribes of Israel. In other words, Paul's mission to the Gentiles was the vehicle whereby the northern tribes would be gathered from exile, reconciled, and restored with the southern kingdom of Judah in the land. By extension, those who had always been outside the covenant would also be reconciled to the Lord. In this way, Israel, as God's special heralds, was the nucleus of the Lord's plan to save all of humanity. Accordingly, they were the chosen and elected vessel that was predestined to bring the good news of reconciliation, restoration, and redemption to the whole world. It was through Israel's restoration promises, fulfilled in Christ in the first century, that all humanity would become "partakers in their spiritual blessings" or "grafted into their promises" (Rom 11:24; 15:27). Simply put, if Israel's restoration promises remain unfulfilled, then there is no salvation for all humanity.

This understanding goes a long way in solving the lingering eschatological issues surrounding the promises of restoration to both houses of Israel. Additionally, this study will demonstrate that there is a consistent-sovereign narrative unity in the matter of redemptive history. Simply put, Paul's mission to the Gentiles was simultaneously bringing about the restoration and reconciliation of all Israel, and by extension, the whole world.

Chapter 2
PRELIMINARY CONSIDERATIONS

2.1. A Note on Terminology

One recurring problem in any academic dialogue is nomenclature. Often discourse within the guild, whether oral or written, is filled with an abundance of scholarly terms that are not always clearly defined. However, my task in this study is to demonstrate a nuanced understanding of Paul's mission, and not to simply produce a work besieged by potential misunderstandings. Therefore, before we embark on this study, a brief explanation of key terminology is necessary.

2.1.1. Old Testament, Hebrew Bible, Israel's Scripture

In this study, I attempt to reflect the frame of mind of the original author of the text in question (i.e., Rom 9:24–26). Therefore, though I reserve the right to make exceptions to this rule, the term "Israel's Scripture" will primarily be employed when speaking of Paul's use of the Old Testament. Of course, this is not to suggest that Israel's Scriptures correlated precisely with what we might call the Old Testament today. The term "Old Testament" was unquestionably anachronistic to Paul's time. Moreover, there would not have been an "authoritative" text called the "New Testament" in existence during his time. Paul's text was undoubtedly Israel's sacrosanct corpus of texts.

Likewise, the term "Hebrew Bible" would not be suitable, since Paul primarily made use of the Septuagint (LXX) textual tradition and not the Hebrew.⁶¹ Of course, some scholars have convincingly argued that Paul might have employed a Hebrew text in some manner.⁶² Undoubtedly, the apostle likely read Hebrew and Aramaic;⁶³ nonetheless, the Greek of the LXX satisfactorily explains the majority of Paul's quotations, allusions, and echoes. Simply put, the apostle was writing in Greek and using Greek texts because of their importance for the Greek speaking communities to which he was addressing.⁶⁴

2.1.2. Ἰουδαῖος, Ἰσραηλίτης, ἔθνη

One of the central tasks of this study is to demonstrate a terminological meticulousness in the matter of exilic history. With this in mind, the most significant distinction made in this study is between the terms, Ἰουδαῖος ("Jew"), Ἰσραηλίτης ("Israelite"), and ἔθνη ("Gentile").

---

⁶¹ By "the Septuagint" (LXX), I mean the Greek LXX tradition itself. Of course, countless renderings of the LXX have diachronically emerged. In fact, it is highly likely that Paul often utilized revised LXX texts. For more on this, see Wagner, *Heralds*, 16 n.60.

⁶² See e.g., Timothy H. Lim, *Holy Scripture in the Qumran Commentaries and Pauline Letters* (Oxford: Clarendon, 1997).

⁶³ Lim argues that this was likely given Paul's pharisaical training in Jerusalem—see *ibid.*, 161–68.

⁶⁴ Due to restrictions of a study like this, I am required to be quite ephemeral. However, I tend to side with the consensus view that Paul is making use of the LXX tradition. For more on this discussion, see Wagner, *Heralds*, 2003; Christopher Stanley, *Paul and the Language of Scripture: Citation Technique in the Pauline Epistles and Contemporary Literature* (Cambridge: Cambridge University Press, 1992); T. M. Law, *When God Spoke Greek: The Septuagint and the Making of the Christian Bible* (Oxford: Oxford University Press, 2013); Dietrich-Alex Koch, *Die Schrift als Zeuge des Evangeliums: Untersuchungen zur Verwendung und zum Verstandnis der Schrift bei Paulus*, BHT 69 (Tübingen: J.C.B. Mohr [Paul Siebeck], 1986).

As I have already demonstrated in chapter 1, many interpreters have assumed that the terms "Israel" or "Israelite" are to be taken as synonyms for the term "Jew." For example, I have already noted Theodoret's claim that Hos 1:9–10 and 2:23 "originally applied to Jews."[65] Equally, Cottrell's assertion that "these Jews had become 'not loved' and 'not my people' through the judgment of the exile";[66] Cranfield's comment that Paul saw in "the ten lost tribes...a type of the unbelieving majority of his Jewish contemporaries";[67] and finally Wright's abandonment of geographical exile for political (and shall we say theological) exile along with his comment that "most Jews of this period" believed they were "still in exile."[68] The issue with these views is twofold: 1) Hos 1:9–10 and 2:23 are not speaking of the Jews, but of Israelites. More specifically, it is written to the northern tribes of Israel; and 2), the failure to recognize that there were two exiles in Israel's history creates an unwarranted shift in terminology that makes the terms "Israelite" and "Jew" or "the northern tribes of Israel" and "the southern tribes of Judah" identical analogues. However, they are not.

a) Ἰουδαῖος

In academic vernacular the term "Jew" can embody a variety of different meanings. It can be used to convey a religious connotation—e.g., an individual who practices the religion of Judaism. It can also be employed to convey an ethnic or geographic designation. Shaye Cohen notes that before the end of the second century BCE the terms "*Ioudaios* (pl., *Ioudaioi*), Latin *Iudaeus* (pl., *Iudaei*), and Hebrew *Yehudi* (pl., *Yehudim*) [were]

---

[65] Theodoret of Cyrus, *Interpretation* (PG 82.43–226).
[66] Cottrell, *Romans*, 2:134–35.
[67] Cranfield, *Romans*, 2:499–500.
[68] Wright, *New Testament and the People of God*, 268–69.

originally, and in antiquity primarily, ethnic-geographic terms, designating the eponymous inhabitants of the land of *Ioudaia/Yehudah*."⁶⁹ Therefore, he argues, the term *Ioudaios* should be translated as "Judaean," when speaking of this period. Afterwards, *Ioudaios* should be translated as "Jew," because the term underwent a "semantic shift" and came to encompass all those who "believe in the God of the Judaeans" or those who "have become 'Judaeans' in a political sense (i.e., state citizens)."⁷⁰

Moreover, Niels Peter Lemche posits that the term "Jew" became primarily "the name of the post-exilic population that centered on Jerusalem and the worship of YHWH in its temple;"⁷¹ it was not a term for those outside that particular community. Regardless of this distinction, what is certain is that the term Ἰουδαῖος ("Jew") did not exist until the southern kingdom's Babylonian captivity. That is, it is a designation for members of the tribe of Judah and not the northern tribes of Israel. Josephus confirms this when he observes: "the Jews…that is the name they are called by from the day that they came up from Babylon, which is taken from the tribe of Judah."⁷² Moreover, Staples asserts: "the term Ἰουδαῖος is necessarily limited to descendants of the southern kingdom, which were exiled to Babylon and then returned."⁷³ Therefore, in this study, the term "Jew" is never employed as a reference to the whole of Israel. Likewise, it is never used as a reference to the northern tribes of Israel.

---

⁶⁹ Shaye J. D. Cohen, *The Beginnings of Jewishness: Boundaries, Varieties, Uncertainties* (Berkeley: University of California Press, 1999), 69–70.

⁷⁰ *Ibid.*

⁷¹ Niels Peter Lemche, *The A to Z of Ancient Israel* (Lanham: Scarecrow Press, 2010), 168.

⁷² Josephus, *Ant.* 11.173.

⁷³ Staples, "A Fresh Look at Romans 11:25–27," 374–78.

b) Ἰσραηλίτης

It has sometimes been assumed that Second-Temple Jews adopted the term "Israelite" after the fall of the northern kingdom in 722 BCE, thus making the two a homogenous group. For example, Moo claims: "The term *Jew* originally referred to a person from the region occupied by the descendants of Judah, but it was applied generally to Israelite people after the Exile."[74] In other words, he asserts that there is to be no distinction between Israelites and Jews in post-exilic times. One might also point to Paul's own words for the support of Moo's position: "[I am] a member of the people of Israel, of the tribe of Benjamin" (Phil 3:5); "I myself am an Israelite, a descendant of Abraham, a member of the tribe of Benjamin" (Rom 11:1); "Are they Israelites? So am I" (2 Cor 11:22).

However, the problem with Moo's understanding is that it creates an unnecessary shift on the term and fails to consider that the term "Israel" is also used to refer to the grander national entity of Israel. As Staples notes: "To use a modern parallel, a Floridian would surely be called an American when being distinguished from an Australian, but not all Americans are Floridians. In the same manner, the term 'Israel' may—and often does—refer to Jews, though its meaning is not limited to just the Jews."[75]

Thus, in this study, I argue for a distinction between the expressions Israelite and Jew. That is, except for this exception mentioned by Staples, the term Ἰσραηλίτης "Israelite" is primarily used to refer to the northern tribes of Israel. Concerning this division, Niels Peter Lemche writes:

---

[74] Douglas J. Moo, *Romans*, NIVAC (Grand Rapids: Zondervan, 2000), 91 (emphasis original).

[75] Staples, "A Fresh Look at Romans 11:25–27," 375.

> For reasons of clarity, Israelites are the descendants of Jacob, alias Israel, in the Old Testament considered one nation until they were divided after Solomon's death. The distinction applies between the inhabitants of the kingdom of Israel and the kingdom of Judah…and Jews becoming the name of the post-exilic population that centered on Jerusalem and the worship of YHWH in its temple.[76]

Moreover, I agree with Staples, who observes that Josephus supported this same distinctive terminology. That is, Josephus used "Ἰσραηλίτης 188 times in the first eleven books of the *Antiquities*—books dealing with the pre-exilic and exilic periods" and uses "Ἰουδαῖος 1,190 times" mostly in his post-exilic work.[77] Yet again, Staples demonstrates that the *War Scroll* draws on this same terminological exactitude: "'[the southern tribes] the sons of Levi, the sons of Judah, and the sons of Benjamin' [are] to be joined by 'the exiles of the sons of light' in the final apocalyptic battle when everything is set right (1QM 1:2–3)."[78]

I shall say more on the Second-Temple expectation of restoration for the northern tribes in chapter 4. Nevertheless, one thing seems certain: after 930 BCE, when the northern kingdom (i.e., the northern tribes) had gained political independence from the southern kingdom (i.e., Judah), the northern tribes—primarily, but not in all cases—became known as "Israelites" in order to properly differentiate them from the "Jews" in the southern kingdom of Judah.

Before proceeding, one final observation should be made concerning Israelite terminology. In many of ancient Israel's

---

[76] Lemche, *The A to Z of Ancient Israel*, 168.

[77] Staples, "A Fresh Look at Romans 11:25–27," 376 n.23; 376. See also Josephus, *Ant.* 11.173.

[78] Staples, "A Fresh Look at Romans 11:25–27," 377.

prophetic books, "Ephraim" is also employed as a name for the northern tribes of Israel. The exiled northern tribes were Reuben, Shimon, Zebulun, Yissachar, Dan, Gad, Asher, Naphtali, Ephraim, and Manasseh. Jacob, whose name was changed to "Israel," declared that the sons of Joseph—i.e., Ephraim and Manasseh—would perpetuate the name of Israel and "grow into a multitude on the earth" (Gen 48:16). However, it was said of Ephraim's descendants that they would become the fullness of the Gentiles (Gen 48:19 [LXX: πλῆθος ἐθνῶν] [MT: מלא־הגוים]; Rom 11:25b: τὸ πλήρωμα τῶν ἐθνῶν]).[79] Thus, these descendants of Ephraim can also properly be called Israelites or designated as the northern tribes of Israel (more on this in chapter 5).

c) ἔθνη

The term "Gentile" (MT: גוי) is often understood as a term that represents only non-Israelites. Accordingly, these Gentiles have been perennially viewed as only a detached ethnic group that shares no affinities with the northern tribes of Israel. However, as I will argue in the remainder of this study, in Paul's mind "[the northern tribes/Ephraim] mixed himself among the peoples," and was thus "swallowed up among the nations" [Gentiles], a "useless" or "dishonorable vessel" (Hos 7:8; 8:8; Rom 9:22). So much so, that the northern kingdom's special standing as the covenant people of the Lord was lost and their status was changed to "not my people" (Hos 1:8) or "not loved" (Hos 1:6)—i.e., Gentiles.

2.2. Methodology

An brief survey of the literary critics and their theories will reveal that they were the pioneers who provided the literary catalyst necessary for advancing the theory that certain phrases, metaphors, and figures of speech can only be understood in

---

[79] I give this echo the proper attention in Ch. 5.

relation to their employment of prior texts, and equally, that these can sometimes undergo a literary transmutation into a new literary context.

This particular campaign of literary criticism was progressive in nature. That is, it gradually developed upon previous theories and their presuppositions. Ferdinand de Saussure's "Functional Structuralism" can certainly be pointed to as the first to promote the idea that language consists of a system of "signs" whose meaning is only determined by observing the relationship between the "signifier" and the "signified."[80] These signs have no meaning outside of their own system of context. Roland Barthes's "Structural Narrative Analysis" must also be noted. This method looked for a system of relations within the particular narratives.[81] Moreover, I would be remiss if I did not mention A.J. Greimas's "Repetitious Isotopy." It demonstrated that a narrative often contains the recurrence of "seme," which serves to bring a proper framework and familiarity to its meaning.[82] Similarly, Mikhail Bakhtin's "Dialogism" contends that language is formed in the process of social interaction in which new words are determined through the perception of earlier ones.[83] Correspondingly, Julia Kristeva's *"Intertextualité"* was the idea that "in the space of a

---

[80] Ferdinand de Saussure, *Course in General Linguistics,* trans. Wade Baskin; eds. Charles Bally and Albert Reidlinger (New York: Philosophical Library, 1959), 65.

[81] For a deeper explanation, see Susan Sontag, ed., *A Barthes Reader* (New York: Hill and Wang, 1982).

[82] See A. J. Greimas and Joseph Courtés, *Semiotics and Language an Analytical Dictionary* (Bloomington: Indiana University Press, 1982).

[83] M. M. Bakhtin, *The Dialogic Imagination: Four Essays*, trans. Caryl Emerson and Michael Holquist; ed. Michael Holquist (Austin: University of Texas Press, 1981), 426. See also P. N. Medvedev and M. M. Bakhtin, *The Formal Method in Literary Scholarship: A Critical Introduction to Sociological Poetics*, trans. Albert J. Wehrle (Baltimore: Johns Hopkins University Press, 1978), xi.

given text, several utterances, taken from other texts, intersect and neutralize one another."[84] In my view, Kristeva's literary approach is one that has most drastically advanced linguistic semiosis. Finally, John Hollander's suggestion of "Transumption" or "Metalepsis" (to whom Hays's work is indebted) must be mentioned. Hollander defines this as "a highly allusive situation, in which an image or fable is being presented as a revision of an earlier one."[85] His literary method suggests that "echoes" are heard, then infused into the writer's own contemporary text from an earlier writing.[86] According to Hollander, "the revisionary power of allusive echo generates a new figuration."[87] It is this approach that has continued to experience a metamorphosis in biblical scholarship since its initial mutation.

2.2.1. *Inner-Biblical Exegesis and the Phenomenon of Intertextuality*

Michael Fishbane's "Inner-Biblical Exegesis"[88] and Hays's "Phenomenon of Intertextuality"[89] are directly responsible for the sustained hegemonistic success of intertextual analysis in the field of biblical studies. In my research, I have found these to be some of the most noteworthy developments in literary critical theory.

---

[84] See Julia Kristeva, *Desire in Language: a Semiotic Approach to Literature and Art*, ed. Leon S. Roudiez (New York: Columbia University Press, 1980), 36; Toril Moi, ed., *The Kristeva Reader* (New York: Columbia University Press, 1986). Kristeva was the first to coin the term "intertextuality."

[85] John Hollander, *The Figure of Echo: A Mode of Allusion in Milton and After* (Berkeley: University of California Press, 1981), 114.

[86] *Ibid.*, 133–49.

[87] *Ibid.*, ix.

[88] Michael A. Fishbane, *Biblical Interpretation in Ancient Israel* (Oxford: Clarendon, 1985). See also idem, "Inner-Biblical Exegesis" in *Hebrew Bible, Old Testament: The History of Its Interpretation*, vol. 1; ed. Magne Saebo (Göttingen: Vandenhoeck & Ruprecht, 1996), 33–48.

[89] Hays, *Echoes*, 14.

Fishbane asserts that Israel's Scripture diachronically underwent some revisionary hermeneutical methods, in that within them they contain: "a vast range of annotations, adaptations, and comments on earlier traditions."[90] However, more specific to this study is Hays's method, which emphasizes that Paul's letters are "shaped by complex intertextual relations with [Israel's] Scripture."[91] That is, in Paul's writings we find "the imbedding of fragments of an earlier text."[92] Therefore, this study will give prominence to the task of analyzing the "imbedding" of Israel's Scripture in Paul's first-century writing. In doing so, this study stands upon the shoulders of scholars such as Fishbane and Hays.

2.2.2. Hays: Echo, Allusion, and Quotations

This "imbedding of fragments" is commonly referred to as "intertextual echo."[93] Hays has often been criticized for employing "echo" as an umbrella term for the "phenomenon of intertextuality."[94] More specifically, it has been pointed out that in his book, *Echoes of Scripture in the Letters of Paul*, he often conflated the two terms "allusion" and "echo."[95] Nevertheless, there is a slight difference. Thus, it is necessary to divide the procedure of intertextuality into three distinctive foci:

---

[90] Fishbane, "Inner-Biblical Exegesis," 35.

[91] Hays, *Echoes*, xi.

[92] *Ibid.*, 14.

[93] *Ibid.*

[94] Stanley E. Porter, "Allusions and Echoes," in *As It Is Written: Studying Paul's Use of Scripture*, eds. Stanley E. Porter and Christopher D. Stanley (Atlanta: Society of Biblical Literature, 2008), 29–30; cf. also idem, "The Use of the Old Testament in the New Testament: A Brief Comment on Method and Terminology," in *Early Christian Interpretation of the Scriptures of Israel Investigations and Proposals*, eds. Craig A. Evans and James A. Sanders (Sheffield: Sheffield Academic, 1997).

[95] Porter, "Allusions and Echoes," 34–35.

1. <u>Quotations</u>, especially in Pauline texts, are easily identifiable as they are usually cited verbatim from the LXX.
2. <u>Allusions</u> are those obvious intertextual references, which are not in all ways complete quotations, nor are they as faint as echoes. They are unambiguous, explicit, and intentional on the part of the author; yet simultaneously, they do not always draw a direct connection between the two texts. Instead, allusions rely upon the reader's textual vocabulary.
3. <u>Echoes</u> are "subtler" intertextual references,[96] distinguished from allusions. Thus, echoes are: sometimes implicit with no corresponding qualification; sometimes unspoken or unwritten, but yet, still insinuated; deeply woven into the very fabric of Paul's thought, and thus never quoted verbatim; and less precise than allusions and frequently very faint, because for the writer (in this case, Paul) it might be on some level an unconscious act—i.e., something that emerges from a mind suffused in the Scriptures of ancient Israel.

2.2.3. Hays's Seven Criteria

It is precisely because echoes are not synonymous with allusions that we must adopt a criterion for determining the tenability of any claim. Thus, I will primarily assume the hermeneutical methods of detection first set forth by Hays by considering the following:

1. <u>Availability</u>: "Was the proposed source of the echo available to the author and/or original readers?"[97] As I

---

[96] Hays, *Echoes*, 29.
[97] *Ibid.*, 29–30.

pointed out earlier, it is highly likely that Paul often utilized a body of revised LXX texts. Therefore, it is also highly likely that his readers shared in that same knowledge.[98] Again, as I mentioned earlier, the apostle Paul was writing in Greek and likely using these texts because of their importance for the Greek speaking communities to which he was addressing.

2. <u>Volume</u>: "The volume of an echo is determined primarily by the degree of explicit repetition of words or syntactical patterns."[99] However, Hays, in a separate work, has further nuanced this rule as: "how insistently the echo presses itself upon the reader?"[100] This of course depends upon the vocabulary of the reader and the "popular familiarity of the precursor text."[101] That is, the question must be asked: "How familiar would have the proposed echo have been within Second-Temple Judaism?"[102] If familiar, then it would have most likely served as a verbal cue in the ear of the reader.

3. <u>Recurrence</u>: "How often does Paul elsewhere cite or allude to the same scriptural passage?"[103]

4. <u>Thematic Coherence</u>: "How well does the alleged echo fit into the line of argument that Paul is developing?"[104]

5. <u>Historical Plausibility</u>: "Could Paul have intended the alleged meaning effect? Could his readers have understood it?"[105]

---

[98] For a deeper discussion see Wagner, *Heralds*, 1–13.
[99] *Ibid.*, 31.
[100] Hays, *Conversion*, 36.
[101] *Ibid.*
[102] Hays, *Echoes*, 30.
[103] *Ibid.*
[104] *Ibid.*
[105] *Ibid.*

6. History of Interpretation: "Have other readers, both critical and pre-critical, heard the same echoes?"[106]
7. Satisfaction: "With or without clear confirmation from the other criteria listed here, does the proposed reading make sense?"[107] In chapter five, I will demonstrate the application of these criteria to the particular instance of intertextuality in question—i.e., Paul's appropriation of Hos 1:9–10 and 2:23 in Rom 9:24–26.

2.2.4. Narrative Intertextuality

Another prominent aspect of this intertextual method is the development of "narrative intertextuality," previously known as "narrative structuralism."[108] Effectively, this is a metamorphosis in the work of earlier literary critics. Here, Hays must also be acknowledged for his keen exegetical acumen, specifically his contribution to narrative criticism. It was under the direction of William A. Beardslee that Hays wrote his dissertation while a student at Emory University, in which he argued—among other things[109]—that a "discourse exists and has meaning only as an unfolding of the meaning of the story."[110] In other words, Hays hypothesizes that there is a "narrative substructure" that lies underneath the text and within Paul's theological reflection, one that provides the proper framework for understanding and interpreting his theology.

---

[106] *Ibid.*, 31.

[107] *Ibid.*, 31–32.

[108] A term initially coined by Roland Barthes. For a deeper discussion, see Sontag, *A Barthes Reader*.

[109] Hays' dissertation and later book was the catalyst for the "πίστεως Ἰησοῦ Χριστοῦ" debate—i.e., is it objective or subjective genitive? See Richard B. Hays, *The Faith of Jesus Christ: An Investigation of the Narrative Substructure of Galatians 3:1–4:11*, SBLDS 56 (Chico: Scholars Press, 1983).

[110] *Ibid.*, 22.

Moreover, building upon Hays' contribution, Sylvia Keesmaat has argued that Paul is not entirely concerned with a complete unequivocal or unambiguous retelling of Israel's story. Instead, Paul relies on his own reflections of Israel's narrative to frame his theology.[111] Thus, Paul is not always recalling a particular text, but often a portion of the narrative itself—hence, *metalepsis*. Therefore, when searching for intertextual echoes in Paul's writings, the exegete should not always limit them to precise word-for-word quotations:

> Paul's echoes and allusions...occur within a larger matrix of ideas. [They] most often occur in a narrative context.... The intertextual matrix upon which Paul draws is not just a cluster of motifs and themes, which jostled around with one another in the collective mind of first-century Judaism. This matrix is actually a larger story, told and retold in past remembrance and future hope to shape Israel's identity and future expectation. The reinterpreted memories of this story provide a vision of the future, which revivifies the tradition in the present.[112]

In addition to Keesmaat, Wright has also followed Hays's method of exegesis. Paul's theology is "not an ahistorical scheme about how individuals come into a right relationship with God, but rather tells [a story about] how the God of Abraham has fulfilled his promises at last through the apocalyptic death and resurrection of

---

[111] As in Keesmaat's explanation of the Exodus narrative—see "Exodus and the Intertextual Transformation of Tradition in Romans 8:14-30," *JSNT* 54 (1994): 29–56.

[112] Sylvia Keesmaat, "Paul and his Story," in *Early Christian Interpretation of the Scriptures of Israel Investigations and Proposals*, eds. Craig A. Evans and James A. Sanders (Sheffield: Sheffield Academic, 1997), 319.

his own beloved Son."[113] Moreover, it is about "how the plot was progressing and, perhaps, reaching its climax."[114] Furthermore, Wright argues that in the Second-Temple period:

> [S]cripture itself was seen not simply as a rag-bag, a miscellaneous collection of texts from which one might summon up a maxim, an example, a historical insight, a 'type' or whatever. All of those are of course there in profusion. But they are seen...in terms of the *overall* narrative within which the second-Temple reader was presumed to be living.[115]

Therefore, with this in mind, one task in this study is to show that those echoes, allusions, or quotations found in Paul's appropriation of Hos 1:9–10 and 2:23 in Rom 9:24–26 are not the result of some capricious proof-texting on Paul's behalf. Instead, they are employed to evoke the promise of Israel's restoration as a robust metanarrative in Paul's efforts toward Jewish and Gentile reconciliation.

2.3. Procedure

With the nuances of these methods in mind, I will conduct my analysis of Rom 9:24–26 by locating this study against the backdrop of these well-established intertextual methods. I shall make my case with the support of the following foci:

1. I will conduct a brief analysis of the OT context with the intent to reveal analogous structural characteristics.

---

[113] Wright, *Paul: In Fresh Perspectives*, 10.
[114] *Ibid.*, 12.
[115] Wright, *Paul and the Faithfulness of God*, 175 (emphasis original).

2. Additionally, I will conduct a textual comparison primarily against the textual tradition defined above (LXX) and with variant readings in the MS tradition of the LXX when relevant. I employ this procedure with for the purpose of revealing synonymous wording, thus signaling possible quotation, allusions, and echoes.
3. In addition to the LXX, when relevant, I will compare our Hosean passage against the other known textual traditions such as the MT. This is done in an effort to identify other possible implications for our study.
4. When pertinent, I will conduct an analysis will using Hays's "seven criteria."[116]
5. Finally, I will devote considerable space to examining the narrative structure between the texts in question. Here, my own exegesis will interact, to varying degrees, with the narrative structuralism of Hays, Keesmaat, and Wright.

2.3.1. Sources

In order to make this case as objective as possible, I will support these five foci with Second-Temple literary sources from between 300 BCE and 70 CE. This textual pool includes, but is not limited to: Josephus, significant pseudepigraphal writings, and non-canonical Dead Sea Scroll material (e.g., 1QM, 4Q174, 4Q385, 4Q386, and 4Q388). While examining these sources, I am seeking to answer the question: "What were the restoration and exile expectations of those living in the Second-Temple period?" Likewise, an examination of these sources will enable us to look for a reading of Hos 1:9–10 and 2:23 that either bolsters or undermines my overall thesis. This is accomplished not just by looking at the history of what biblical historians may already

---

[116] Hays, *Echoes*, 29–32. Quotations are easily identifiable. Thus, it is only necessary to apply Hays's criterion to possible allusions and echoes.

know, but also by ascertaining the scope and significance of restoration from exile interpretations for *all twelve tribes of Israel* (i.e., not just Judah) within the Second-Temple Period.

2.4. Hermeneutical Issues and Assumptions

In this study, I will seek to uncover the hermeneutical logic that guides Paul's appropriation of Hos 1:9–10 and 2:23 in Rom 9:24–26. This means, I am wholly committed to the idea that it is still possible to retrieve Paul's authorial intent.

Of course, this claim is becoming less popular within the halls of biblio-academia. Since the advent of postmodern methods of biblical interpretation, the exegetical analysis of any text by many biblical scholars has moved away from this specific motivation. Simply put, for many scholars, authorial intent is now a moot point. The emphasis now is that there are multiple other ways of interpreting the text, and that meaning is only found in the eye of the beholder. Therefore, many interpreters have endeavored to make sense of Paul's text in other ways. For example, cultural-feminist critics seek to point out in Paul those parts that are against women, and thus feel the feminist perspective on Paul has been mildly underrepresented.[117] That is, it is suggested that in the Pauline corpus, there are patterns of thought that define women as subordinate to men, and these have helped "to promote prejudice and sexism against women in our modern society."[118] Another example would be scholars who prefer to read Paul's narrative with a "liberating praxis" in mind,[119] exposing the "evident racism

---

[117] Amy-Jill Levine and Marianne Blickenstaff, eds., *A Feminist Companion to Paul* (Cleveland, OH: Pilgrim, 2004).

[118] Elisabeth Fiorenza Schüssler, *In Memory of Her: A Feminist Reconstruction of Christian Origins* (London: SCM, 1995).

[119] Ada Maria Isasi-Diaz, "By the Rivers of Babylon: Exile as a Way of Life," in *Reading from this Place*, vol. 1; eds. Fernado F. Segovia and Mary Ann Tolbert (Minneapolis: Fortress, 1995), 151.

in Paul's text (e.g., Philemon)" through an "African American liberationist reading."[120] Finally, Marxist literary critics argue that within Paul's texts, attention should be given to its "socio-economic substructure" or to the obvious "class conflict" between the "oppressors and oppressed; the rulers and ruled."[121]

In our modern academic climate, scriptural interpretation has largely become centered on these modern issues of socio-economic justice for the oppressed, poor, minority, and marginalized in society. My point is not that these perspectives are of no use, but that one unfortunate consequence of our focus on gender, social, and intercultural hermeneutics (i.e., subsets of reader-response criticism, deconstructionism, and post-colonialism) is that in our efforts to be a "voice for the marginalized,"[122] we have rendered the text completely indeterminate and thereby marginalized anyone with a keen interest in discovering authorial intent.

I do not wish to be misunderstood. Complete objectivity is indeed a myth. However, it has become customary to suggest that the "meaning of every text is [only] found in the relationship that is created between the reader, the writer, and the text," i.e., the meaning is "completely" dependent upon the interpreter and not the author.[123] My point is that we must exercise caution when considering this suggestion. An unfortunate consequence of the

---

[120] Randall C. Bailey, "The Danger of Ignoring One's Own Cultural Bias in Interpreting the Text," in *The Postcolonial Bible*, ed. R.S. Sugirtharajah (Sheffield: Sheffield Academic, 1998), 66–99.

[121] Roland Boer, *Marxist Criticism of the Bible* (London: T&T Clark International, 2003); Gerd Theissen, *The Social Setting of Pauline Christianity: Essays on Corinth*, trans. John H. Schütz (Edinburgh: T&T Clark, 1982).

[122] See, e.g., Musa W. Dube. "Reading for Decolonization (John 4.1–42)," in *John and Postcolonialism: Travel, Space and Power*, eds. Musa W. Dube and Jeffrey L. Staley (Sheffield: Sheffield Academic, 2005), 51–75.

[123] This is a typical definition of Reader-Response Criticism—see Isasi-Diaz, "By the Rivers of Babylon," 151.

guild's move in this direction has been that it has somewhat diminished the importance of authorial intent, along with the author's cultural and historical background. In fact, as I have already pointed out, it has largely been built upon the premise that authorial intent is not recoverable.

My own exegesis of Rom 9:24–26 moves away from the premise that the reader gives the text its meaning. Though I think postmodernism has rightly challenged many of the theoretical assumptions and untenable premises of modernity along with its rationalistic philosophy, I also think it has negatively shifted the interpreter's concern too far away from the historical world that lies behind the text; and thus, has created an even worst state of theoretical flux. For now, I am still under the conviction—maybe naively so, since so many post-critical scholars have abandoned the idea—that the intended authorial meaning of the text is indeed recoverable. However, I also readily admit that this undoubtedly depends upon the reader's familiarity with the author's library, but this fact does not necessitate that the reader provide meaning.

I also argue that certain instruments of both historical and literary criticism are useful for such an enterprise. These are simply analytical tools, and they are not in and of themselves inherently biased. Instead, it is often the practitioners who lack a sense of objectivity and often have ideological axes to grind. However, in saying this, I am not suggesting that freedom from interpretive bias is completely obtainable, only that there are tools in place to make us aware of our own ideological axes. Nevertheless, my primary fear is that we are losing sight of the sacred text itself. Thus, my underlying premise in this study is that authorial intent is indeed recoverable by reading the text in a way that brings unity of meaning to both the historical context and the story within the text.

To read the biblical texts as stories is to employ narrative criticism. Likewise, to read the biblical texts with a concern for recovering "authorial intent" or "intended meaning" is to employ historical-criticism. Thus, throughout this study, my hermeneutical approach is *historical-narrative* in nature. A historical-narrative approach is particularly interested in restoring the narrative dimensions of the text by demonstrating that the original author was creatively retelling Israel's story to elicit a simultaneous historical and contemporary significance in the mind of the ancient hearer.

2.4.1. Paul's History and Hermeneutic: What is Paul Doing with Israel's Scripture?

As I have already mentioned, a number of biblical scholars rightly observe that no human writer has ever approached the task of writing with a set of "neutral" or "objective" presuppositions in mind. In the case of Paul's gospel, he has a strong opinion about what he thinks is Jesus's significance as Israel's long-awaited Messiah (e.g., Rom 1:1–3; 9–11; Gal 2:16). That is, Paul saw Jesus as the true Messiah promised to Israel, thus his writings contain a very high Christology (Rom 10:4).[124] Therefore, it can be said that Paul desired to create a "theological narrative," which had immediate significance for his own contemporaries as an exemplary catalyst for eliciting faith.

With this in mind, it must also be understood that Paul is not necessarily attempting to provide an "accurate" history per se, nor a "chronological" account of Jesus's life and events. That is, the biblical authors were not, in every case, interested in creating a historically pristine record of things; rather, they were seeking to

---

[124] For a thorough examination of Paul's Christology, see Chris Tilling, *Paul's Divine Christology* (Tübingen: Mohr Siebeck, 2012).

provide a narrative that incorporates both selective and relevant pieces of information from the past.

Of course, since the Enlightenment, an amalgamation of biblical criticism and biblical archaeology has demonstrated to us that the biblical narrative does not always reflect an accurate chronological historiography. In the case of Paul's writing, it is important for the interpreter to be cognizant of the process of history-development in the writer's narrative. That is, it is the writer's particular theological perspective that often serves as an aid in how he decides which portions of or events in history to include or exclude. Thus, it is a conglomeration of both history and theology that ultimately shapes the telling of the apostle's story. That is, it is often a blend of history and theology interacting with each other throughout Paul's narrative.

This unembellished interaction between history and theology in creating narrative was commonplace in late Second-Temple writing. That is, there was sometimes a lack of concern for pristine historical accuracy, and more of a concern for the meaning that the author was able to acquire from his sources for contemporary significance. As James Greer and Rowan Kugal have said:

> [T]he past was not approached in the spirit of antiquarianism but for what message it might yield, and this is necessarily predicated on an interpretive stance, indeed, a willingness to deviate from the texts' plain sense. The words of prophets, the accounts of ancient historians, were to be "translated" into present-day significance, referred to (and sometimes distorted) in order to support a particular view of the present, or a program for the future.[125]

---

[125] James L. Kugel and Rowan A. Greer, *Early Biblical Interpretation*, ed. Wayne A. Meeks (Philadelphia: Westminster, 1986), 38.

While I agree with Greer and Kugal that "the past was not [always] approached in the spirit of antiquarianism," I take issue with the insinuation that the biblical writers (i.e., in this case Paul) deviated from the text's "plain sense." Instead, the writers were both creatively and artistically telling a story in a way that would recall a much older story, thereby contributing to the overall metanarrative. By employing selective parts of history and excluding others, the writers were able to place the plot and characters of the narrative in a specific setting that was significant to the contemporary reader. As Andreas Köstenberger and Richard Patterson have pointed out:

> [N]arratives appear in dramatic form, that is, as *stories* that are presented by the biblical writer with a view toward driving home the significance of a given biblical event or series of events. In this regard, it is important to remember that these stories, in turn, typically contain historical *accounts* of speeches and dialogues that comprise the scenes or episodes which together make up the full story. Indeed, dialogues often form crucial points in a given narrative.[126]

In either case, it is these historical accounts that support and carry the writer's narrative and not necessarily an actual history.

As we shall see in the next chapter of this study, this is a necessary realization as it is typical to hear arguments over the actual identity of the Samaritans—i.e., are they half-Jewish, Israelite, or Gentile? Likewise, some scholars quibble over the degree to which *assyrianized* Israelites were allowed to carry on

---

[126] Andreas J. Köstenberger and Richard D. Patterson, *Invitation to Biblical Interpretation: Exploring the Hermeneutical Triad of History, Literature, and Theology* (Grand Rapids: Kregel, 2011), 238–39—emphasis original.

specific culture practices. However, these do not undermine my thesis. The point of the writer's narrative (i.e., specifically Paul's) is that these groups are outside the covenant promises or the covenant community of God—a problem soon to be remedied by Israel's Messiah. Thus, I contend that a narrative approach can communicate history in such a manner that it is faithful to the critical significance of both history past and the present. As Craig Blomberg has pointed out, the writer's narrative is only "factually accurate within the range of literary and historiographical freedom recognized in the ancient Mediterranean world."[127] In fact, an example of the process Blomberg highlights (i.e., the recasting of a narrative) is found in the following words from 2 Maccabees:

> For considering the flood of statistics involved and the difficulty there is for those who wish to enter upon the narratives of history because of the mass of material, we have aimed to please those who wish to read, to make it easy for those who are inclined to memorize, and to profit all readers. For us who have undertaken the toil of abbreviating, it is no light matter but calls for sweat and loss of sleep, just as it is not easy for one who prepares a banquet and seeks the benefit of others. Nevertheless, to secure the gratitude of many we will gladly endure the uncomfortable toil, *leaving the responsibility for exact details to the compiler, while devoting our effort to arriving at the outlines of the condensation.* For as the master builder of a new house must be concerned with the whole construction, while the one who undertakes its painting and decoration has to consider only what is suitable for its adornment, such in my judgment is the case with us. *It is*

---

[127] Craig Blomberg, *The Historical Reliability of John's Gospel: Issues & Commentary* (Downers Grove, IL: InterVarsity, 2002), 66.

> *the duty of the original historian to occupy the ground, to discuss matters from every side, and to take trouble with details, but the one who recasts the narrative should be allowed to strive for brevity of expression and to forego exhaustive treatment."* (2 Macc 2:24–31—emphasis added)

Thus, in summary, what I am concerned with for the purposes of this study is Paul's interpretation of history. That is, history as he both saw it and shaped it into his telling of the story of Israel (i.e., both Israelite and Jewish), and its concern with Gentile reconciliation. However, before we can examine how he used history to shape his own theology (and vice versa), we must discuss what the apostle might have been considering.

Chapter 3
THE NORTHERN TRIBES OF ISRAEL

3.1. The Issue of Historicity in the Book of Kings

There has been much discussion in the world of biblical scholarship—esp. among Hebrew Bible scholars—as to whether the biblical narrative in the Book of Kings accurately represents the forces that gave shape to both the emergence and demise of the two kingdoms of Israel. Since the days of Graf and Wellhausen, many critical scholars maintain that much of the Hebrew Bible's narrative is the evolutionary product of multiple redactors. That is, the biblical narrative is actually the consequence of a series of addenda placed upon the original stories to aid in retaining Jewish national identity, both in the midst of and following the horror of exile.[128]

Likewise, both twentieth and twenty-first century archeological and textual discoveries have yielded problematic results that are not always easy to reconcile with the biblical narrative. For example, the Hebrew Bible's depiction of the throne succession

---

[128] The Graf-Wellhausen hypothesis considers the Pentateuch a product of four independent narratives, which later were synthesized by redactors (JEDP), who retained what was suitable for their own agendas. Today, many critical scholars have moved away from this scheme and have adopted the "Supplementary Approach." This is a method, which sees much of the Hebrew Bible narrative as an "evolutionary development," i.e., the product of sequential addenda upon the initial stories. For the Graf-Wellhausen hypothesis see, Julius Wellhausen, *Prolegomena zur Geschichte Israels*, 6 ed. (Berlin: Druck und Verlag von G. Reimer, 1905). For a specific discussion on the Supplementary Approach see, Jacob L. Wright, *David, King of Israel, and Caleb in Biblical Memory* (New York: Cambridge University Press, 2014), 11–12; 226.

sequence—i.e., from Saul, to David, to Solomon, and the division of the two kingdoms—are thought by both archeologists and biblical scholars to be fictional narratives. Particularly, the biblical account of Saul and David are thought to be originally the product of two independent narratives. Thus, it has been suggested that the succession narrative was the creation of a redactor, who tried to resolve contradictions between the two supposed competing stories diachronically for the sake of retaining national identity after the exile.[129] The famed inscription on the walls of Karnack temple, along with a broken stele found in Megiddo provides some support to this view. They both speak of the Egyptian ruler Sheshonq and his campaign into the central hill country of the Levant c. 930 BCE. According to the biblical narrative, his main objective was to seize the wealth that Solomon had accrued in Jerusalem (cf. 1 Kgs 14:25–26). However, the archeological evidence, which mentions the places conquered, lacks any reference to Jerusalem. Many scholars suggest that if there was any power in the region that could show military resistance, the Egyptian scribes would have most certainly had mentioned it.[130] Moreover, concerning the northern kingdom of Israel, instead of Jeroboam, Nadab, Baasha, Elah, or Zimri, scholars posit that it was likely the Omride Dynasty (i.e., Omri, Ahab, and Joram) that was responsible for putting the northern kingdom of Israel on the map, thereby moving its capital

---

[129] For a deeper discussion see Wright, *David*, 31–50 (cf. also 226); William G. Dever, *What Did the Biblical Writers Know and When Did They Know It?: What Archaeology Can Tell Us about the Reality of Ancient Israel* (Grand Rapids: Eerdmans, 2001), 32.

[130] Israel Finkelstein and Neil Asher Silberman, *The Bible Unearthed Archaeology's New Vision of Ancient Israel and the Origin of Sacred Texts* (New York: Free Press, 2001), 161.

to Samaria sometime during the ninth century BCE.[131] For example, the Mesha Stele tells us that Moab was oppressed by King Omri and required to pay tribute. Thus, Hebrew Bible scholars and archeologists argue that this provides evidence that the Omri Dynasty significantly expanded the northern kingdom, thus asserting significant military and political influence in the region.[132]

Nonetheless, these examples—whether one is a minimalist or maximalist[133]—have taught us that the biblical narrative in the Hebrew Bible cannot always be treated as an accurate chronological history (i.e., as I have noted in the previous chapter). In spite of this, however, though the biblical narrative in the Book of Kings is understood by many within the guild to have been both redacted and suffused with much later interpolation, biblical scholars and archeologists have accepted specific elements of Israel's narrative as an authentic representation. It is upon this agreed representation that I will begin to build my case.

Furthermore, if it is indeed a blend of both history and theology interacting with one another throughout Paul's narrative, then we can deduce that there were both historical and theological backdrops to his reflection. That is, in Paul, the actual historical defeats and the expectation of the restoration of Israel are theologized into his narrative, especially seen in his use of the

---

[131] For more on this see Joel Baden, *The Historical David: The Real Life of an Invented Hero* (New York: HarperOne, 2013), 43–82; Wright, *David*, 226; Dever, *What Did the Biblical Writers Know*, 32.

[132] *Ibid*.

[133] In twenty-first century biblical scholarship, overall dialogue over historicity has taken place under the two terms "maximalism" and "minimalism." Maximalists accept that most of what is recorded in the Hebrew Bible narrative is actual true history, while minimalist do not automatically assume historical accuracy unless it is first established to be so, by empirical evidence or data (archaeological, extra-biblical, etc.).

restoration-from-exile motif. Therefore, it is not only important to discuss the latter (i.e., Paul's *theological* backdrop—as I shall do in chapters 4 and 5), but also to elaborate further on the former (i.e., Paul's *historical* backdrop).

3.2. The Northern Tribes and Samaria Swallowed up Among the Gentiles

The Assyrian King, Tiglath-Pileser III, spent most of his years between 745–727 BCE conquering the territory and kingdoms of the Levant. Initially, most of the kings of Israel, who reigned from 787–747 BCE, were subservient to Assyria. The official imperial records attest to the continual tribute they paid as a vassal kingdom.[134] In fact, King Menachem (746–737 BCE) also began by showing loyalty to Assyria, thus paying "a thousand talents of silver" in order to maintain the northern kingdom's independence (2 Kgs 15:19–20).[135] However, in 733–732 BCE, the states of the Levant formed a coalition against Assyria led by King Rezin of Aram-Damascus and Pekah, King of Israel (2 Kgs 16:5–9). In the process they provoked Judah, possibly in order to entice them to join in the revolt (2 Kgs 16:5–9). However, the King of Judah at the time—Ahaz—responded by summoning the help of Tiglath-Pileser III, who promptly came and annihilated Aram-Damascus, thus seizing control of the northern territories of Israel. This effectively reduced the northern kingdom of Israel to a fairly insignificant nation surrounding the city of Samaria.

---

[134] As attested to on the Iran-Stela: "Rezin, the Damascene, Menahem, the Samarian, Tuba'il, the Tyrian, etc...I imposed on them tribute of silver, gold, tin, iron, elephant hides, elephant tusks (ivory), blue-purple and red-purple garments, multi-colored garments, camels, and she-camels." ("The Iran Stela," [*COS* 2.117B, 287; trans. K. Lawson Younger]).

[135] Also see, "Summary Inscription 4," (*COS*, 2.117C: 288; trans. K. Lawson Younger).

Shortly thereafter—whether by Sargon II or Hoshea[136]—King Pekah was killed. His replacement, King Hoshea, continued to pay a yearly tribute until the death of Tiglath-Pileser III in 727 BCE, after which he attempted a revolt with the help of Egypt. Later, Shalmaneser V responded by besieging Samaria for several months, but he died soon after, possibly causing a brief retreat.[137]

The final deathblow was dealt in 721–720 BCE, when Sargon II captured the city and brought the northern kingdom of Israel to an end (2 Kgs 18:9–10). Ultimately, Sargon II reports that he made an imperial province of Samaria:

> [The man of Sa]maria, who with a king [hostile to] me had consorted together not to do service and not to bring tribute—and they did battle in the strength of the great gods, my lords I clashed with them. [2]7,280 people with [their] chariots and the gods their trust, as spoil I count, 200 chariots (as) my [royal] muster. I mustered from among them the rest of them I caused to take their dwelling in the midst of Assyria. The city of Samaria I restored, and

---

[136] It is not clear whether Tiglath-Pileser III's description matches the biblical narrative. The annals may credit Tiglath-Pileser III for killing Pekah other than Hoshea. There is a problem with the wording on line 17 in a portion of Tiglath-Pileser III's annals from the fragmentary "Summary Inscription 4." "[I/they killed] Pekah, their king, and I installed Hoshea [as king] over them." See K. Lawson Younger, "The Deportations of the Israelites," *JBL* 117.2 (1998): 201–27.

[137] There continues to be a debate over which Assyrian king actually captured Samaria, as 2 Kgs 17 is a bit equivocal. However, the consensus is that Sargon II was the most prominent king responsible for the Assyrian deportation and repopulation program in Samaria. However, it should also be noted that there were both prior and later deportations. For example, the Assyrian kings: Tiglath-Pileser III (734–732), Sennacherib (705–681), Esarhaddon (681–669), and Ashurbanipal (669–627) also deported people from Palestine. See, *Ant.* 9.277–78.

greater than before I caused it to become. People of lands conquered by my two hands I brought within it; my officer as prefect over them I placed, and together with the people of Assyria I counted them. (Nimrud Prism IV 25–41)[138]

K. Lawson Younger renders the text sharper:

[The inhabitants of Sa]merina, who agreed [and plotted] with a king [hostile to] me, not to endure servitude and not to bring tribute to Assur and who did battle, I fought against them with the power of the great gods, my lords. I counted as spoil 27,280 people, together with their chariots, and gods, in which they trusted. I formed a unit with 200 of [their] chariots for my royal force. I settled the rest of them in the midst of Assyria. I repopulated Samerina more than before. I brought into it people from countries conquered by my hands. I appointed my commissioner as governor over them. And I counted them as Assyrians. (Nimrud Prism IV 25–41)[139]

In the Great Summary Inscription, in reads: "I besieged and conquered Samarina. I took as booty 27,290 people who lived there. I gathered 50 chariots from them, and I taught the rest (of the deportees) their skills. I set my governor over them, and I imposed upon them the (same) tribute as the previous king (Shalmaneser V)."[140]

---

[138] C. J. Gadd, "The Prism Inscriptions of Sargon," *Iraq* 16 (1954): 178–82.

[139] Younger, "Deportations of the Israelites," 216–17.

[140] "The Great Summary Inscription," (*COS* 2.118E: 296–97; trans. K. Lawson Younger). For a discussion of the "27,280/27,290 discrepancy," see Younger, "Deportations of the Israelites," 218.

3.3. Losing Identity: The Assyrian Deportation and Repopulation Program

The most interesting statements in Sargon's report are those that mention his deportation and repopulation efforts: "I repopulated Samerina[141] more than before. I brought into it people from countries conquered by my hands...and I imposed upon them the (same) tribute as the previous king." [142] Customary for subjugating empires of the time, only the social elites and upper class of the population were exiled, as those in positions of power tended to represent a threat to an occupying power. That is, the upper socio-economic classes were seen as wielding the potential influence to organize new uprisings while the poor were not. Thus, the poor typically escaped exile and were charged with keeping the land (e.g., 2 Kgs 25:12). Nevertheless, the exiled were typically repopulated into a previously conquered city. For example, though some from the northern tribes probably fled and assimilated into Judah—evident from immediate population increases in the south—according to the biblical narrative, many of the northern exiles were deported to "Halah, on the Habor, the river of Gozen, and in the cities of the Medes" (2 Kgs 17:6; 18:11).

Josephus seems to concur: "[Shalmaneser V] demolished the government of the Israelites and transplanted all the people into Media and Persia...and when he had removed these people out of this land, he transplanted other nations out of Cuthah...into Samaria" (*Ant.* 9.277–79). Likewise, according to Tiglath-Pileser III's earlier ambiguous mention of his dealings with ancient Israel found in Summary Inscription 4, he had already deported many to Assyria: "I carried off [to] Assyria the land of Bit-Humria (Israel), [...] its 'auxiliary [army/][...] all of its people, [...[I/they killed] Pekah, their king, and I installed Hoshea [as king] over them. I

---

[141] "Samerina" was the Persian name for the region of Samaria.

[142] Younger, "Deportations of the Israelites," 216.

received from them 10 talents of gold, χ talents of silver, [with] their [prop-erty] and [I car]ried them [to Assyria]."[143]

Sargon II tells us that he repopulated Samaria with Arabian Desert tribes: "The Tamudi, Ibadidi, Marsima[ni] and Hajapa, who live in distant Arabia, in the desert, who knew neither overseer nor commander, who never brought tribute to any king; with the help of Assur, my lord, I defeated them. I exiled the rest of them. I settled them in Samerina."[144] Moreover, according to the biblical narrative, the Assyrian kings moved into Samaria other vanquished people groups "from Babylon, Cuthah, Avva, Hamath, and Sepharvaim...*in place of the people of Israel*" (2 Kgs 17:24—emphasis added).

Thus, the *modus operandi* of the Assyrian deportation and repopulation campaign was to affect a shift in personal identity by way of populace amalgamation. For the northern tribes this was accomplished by relocating a "part" of them into a previously conquered land, and the remnants from those preceding vanquished nations into Samaria. Though one goal was to keep the conquered people from recreating former community coherence, it was also a hegemonistic strategy of nation building, by which the population was forced on diverse levels to share in Assyrian identity.

Younger refers to this as "Assyrianization," and emphasizes that it was an essential element to the Assyrian deportation and repopulation program. In other words, it was a concentrated effort to influence the "direction of change...unilaterally toward Assyrian."[145] Although it is difficult to pinpoint a single purpose for this Assyrianization agenda, it is certain that it involved a national

---

[143] "Summary Inscription 4," (*COS*, 2.117C: 288; trans. K. Lawson Younger).

[144] Younger, "Deportations of the Israelites," 226.

[145] *Ibid.*, 224.

and cultural identity change for its subjects. Though it is evident that some Assyrian captives were allowed to carry on specific cultural practices (see *Ant.* 9.288–90), the overall thrust of exile and repopulation was, on diverse levels also, an effort to make the vanquished people groups conform to the ideals and culture of the conquering nation. One example of this effort can be found in Sargon's perennial mention of how he made use of Israelite chariots: "I formed a unit with 200 of [their] chariots for my royal force."[146] Likewise, "I gathered 50 chariots from them."[147] Of this Younger says, "The Assyrian army was truly a multinational force!"[148]

The Assyrian kings often drafted the men of conquered countries for the purpose of creating new military units that would serve to expand the empire's military force. In fact, continually asserted by scholars such as Stephanie M. Dalley and Bob Becking, and reaffirmed by Younger,[149] there is the understanding that many of the inhabitants of Samaria, which were incorporated into the Assyrian army, were in fact deported Israelites:

> Some of the Israelites that were deported by Sargon II in 720 BCE appear to have received preferred treatment, since, as Dalley has argued, the Israelite chariot corps was a desirable entity to the Assyrian military, according to Assyrian administrative documents called the "Horse Lists," which list a unit of Samarian charioteers. While the defense of the empire was shouldered by the very efficient and well-equipped Assyrian army, Assyria's population was

---

[146] *Ibid.*, 216–17.

[147] "The Great Summary Inscription," (*COS* 2.118E: 296–97; trans. K. Lawson Younger).

[148] Younger, "Deportations of the Israelites," 219.

[149] *Ibid.*, 219 n.70.

relatively small and could not provide an army large enough for the needs of its expanding empire. Conscripts from the conquered countries or vassal states commonly filled the ranks. So, in effect, the Assyrian army was a truly multinational force! It is hardly surprising that this practice was particularly widespread during the reigns of Tiglath-Pileser III and Sargon II. In fact, from the published administrative texts, the onomastic evidence shows that "at least one-fifth" of Sargon's army bore West Semitic names. While Dalley's identification of the Samarians listed in the "Horse List" as deported Israelites has been questioned, Sargon's inscriptions clearly show that at least some (sittūti) of the Samarians were treated favorably by Sargon II after the capture and annexation of the city in 720 BCE, being incorporated into the Assyrian army.[150]

Moreover, the phrase "I taught the rest (of the deportees) their skills" found on Sargon's *Prunkinschrift* (i.e., the Great Summary Inscription), seems to speak of some sort of education, or shall I say a re-education program. In fact, a few scholars have pointed out that the phrase: "The people of the four [quarters], of foreign tongue and divergent speech...I made them of one mouth," found on Sargon's Cylinder inscription, is most likely a reference to the forced education of deportees into a common language:[151] "The people of the four [quarters], of foreign tongue and divergent speech, inhabitants of mountain and plain, all whom the Light of the gods, the Lord of all, shepherded, whom I had carried off with my powerful scepter by the command of Assyria, my lord—*I made*

---

[150] *Ibid.*, 219–20.

[151] For a fuller discussion on this, see Hayim Tadmor, "The Aramaization of Assyria: Aspects of Western Impact," *RAI* 25 (Berlin: Dietrich Reimar, 1982), 449–70.

them of one mouth and put them in its midst."[152] On this point, Younger agrees with Hayim Tadmor:

> According to the Cyprus Stela, after the deportation of Harhar, people of other lands previously conquered by Sargon were settled there. 2 Kgs 17:6 and 18:11 demonstrate clearly that the Israelites were one of those peoples. The others very probably included Aramaeans, pre-Iranians, people of Iranian tongues (e.g., Medes), Assyrians, and possibly Luwians from Carchemish. *In such a situation, the only way to survive was to find a common language (obviously Assyrian or perhaps Aramaic in this case), intermarry with everyone else, serve loyally the Assyrian king, do the labor required, adapt other religious deities, and be receptive to other cultural practices.*"[153]

Thus, according to this data, it is evident that Israelite identity was frustrated on diverse levels. However, to us, the specifics as to how much are of little consequence to this study. The point for the purposes of this study is that the Israelites became a people no longer recognized as distinctive. The fact that they were made to share in Assyrian identity on various levels can clearly be substantiated. Of this, Alfred Edersheim has remarked that regardless of the degree to which YHWH worship was retained, much of the northern tribes' identity became "prevailingly heathen":

> The strange mixture of the service of the Lord and foreign rite must have continued. In the course of time the heathen elements would naturally multiply and assume greater

---

[152] Younger, "Deportations of the Israelites," 224 (emphasis added).
[153] *Ibid.*, 223–24 (emphasis added).

prominence, unless, indeed, the people learned repentance by national trials, or from higher teaching. Of this there is not any evidence in the case of Israel; and if the footsteps of these wanderers shall ever be clearly tracked, we expect to find them with a religion composed of various rites, but *prevailingly heathen*, yet with memories of their historical past in traditions, observances, and customs, as well as in names, and bearing the marks of it even in their outward appearance.[154]

3.4. Xenophobic Endogamy and the Northern Tribes as Proto-Samaritans

Surviving conquest was usually dependent upon learning a common language, intermarriage, and especially the ability of the conquered to adapt to other religious and cultural practices (cf. 2 Kgs 17:29–41). Thus, as Younger pointed out, assimilation and intermarriage were highly likely for many of the Assyrian captives. Thus, the data indeed shows that the Israelites were both included in and affected by this integration process. Unlike the Babylonian captives—namely, the returnees to Jerusalem—who were able to retain identity (though not without intermarriage problems of their own), the Assyrian captives were not.[155] In fact, in Ezra 4:4, those

---

[154] Alfred Edersheim, *The History of Israel and Judah: From the Reign of Ahab to the Decline of the Two Kingdoms* (New York: F. H. Revell, 1885), 117 (emphasis added).

[155] Upon returning from Babylon, it was discovered that some had "not separated themselves from the peoples of the lands with their abominations, from the Canaanites, the Hittites, the Perizzites, the Jebusites, the Ammonites, the Moabites, the Egyptians, and the Amorites" (Ezra 9:1). In fact, they had "taken some of their daughters as wives for themselves and for their sons" (Ezra 9:2). Thus, "the holy seed mixed itself with the peoples of the lands" (Ezra 9:2). Moreover, Nehemiah pointed out that: "half of their children spoke the language of Ashdod, and they could not speak the language of Judah, but spoke the

known as the "people of the land" offered to help returning Babylonian captives rebuild "a temple to the Lord" claiming, "We worship your God as you do and we have been sacrificing to him ever since the days of King Esarhaddon of Assyria who brought us here" (Ezra 4:1–2). However, the Babylonian returnees responded by saying, "You shall have no part with us in building a house to our God; but we alone will build to the Lord, the God of Israel, as King Cyrus of Persia has commanded us" (Ezra 4:3).

Though scholars have long recognized the enigmatic identity of these "people of the land," many have suggested that these were proto-Samaritans, or at the very least an amalgamated population of Assyrian vanquished people groups, most likely including intermarried Israelites. For example, H.G.M. Williamson has argued that the phrase "people of the land" is most likely a reference to the Samaritans, which was employed by a redactor during the early Hellenistic Period, "at a time when relations between the two groups [i.e., between the Samaritans and Jews] were strained."[156] Oded Lipschitz posits that the "'adversaries of Judah and Benjamin' and 'the people of the land'…consisted of Israelites who remained in the land and the survivors of the colonies settled under the Assyrians."[157] However, most significant to our study is the fact that Josephus used the biblical account of 2 Kgs 17:25–26—which reflects the conquering of the northern tribes by Assyria—for support that the later Samaritans descended

---

language of various peoples" (Neh 13:24). The solution for both Ezra and Nehemiah was an unsympathetic and xenophobic reinstitution of endogamy, prescribed by the forced divorce of foreign wives (cf. Ezra 10:10; Neh 13:23–30). In the case of those in the priestly lineage, they are required to surrender their credentials as priest (Ezra 10:18–44).

[156] H.G.M. Williamson, *Ezra-Nehemiah*, WBC 16 (Dallas: Word, 1985), 40–41.

[157] Oded Lipschitz, *Judah and the Judeans in the Persian Period* (Winona Lake, IN: Eisenbrauns, 2006), 255.

from those who were subjected to the Assyrian deportation and repopulation program. One particular group that was repopulated into Samaria by the Assyrians was the people from Cuthah. According to Josephus, "Cutheans" was another name for "Samaritans." He observes:

> But now the Cutheans, who removed into Samaria (for that is the name they have been called by to this time, because they were brought out of the country called Cuthah, which is a country of Persia, and there is a river of the same name in it), each of them, according to their nations, which were in number five, brought their own gods into Samaria, and by worshipping them, as was the custom of their own countries, they provoked Almighty God to be angry and displeased at them, for a plague seized upon them, by which they were destroyed; and when they found no cure for their miseries, they learned by the oracle that they ought to worship Almighty God, as the method for their deliverance. So they sent ambassadors to the king of Assyria, and desired him to send them some of those priests of the Israelites whom he had taken captive. And when he thereupon sent them, and the people were by them taught the laws, and the holy worship of God, they worshipped him in a respectful manner, and the plague ceased immediately; and indeed they continue to make use of the very same customs to this very time, and are called in the Hebrew tongue Cutheans, but in the Greek tongue Samaritans. And when they see the Jews in prosperity, they pretend that they are changed, and allied to them, and call them kinsmen, as though they were derived from Joseph, and had by that means an original alliance with them; but when they see them falling into a low condition, they say

they are no way related to them, and that the Jews have no right to expect any kindness or marks of kindred from them, but they declare that they are sojourners, that come from other countries. (*Ant.* 9.288–91)

Likewise, the biblical narrative tells the story as follows:

> The king of Assyria brought people from Babylon, Cuthah, Avva, Hamath, and Sepharvaim, and placed them in the cities of Samaria in place of the people of Israel; they took possession of Samaria, and settled in its cities. When they first settled there, they did not worship the Lord; therefore the Lord sent lions among them, which killed some of them. So the king of Assyria was told, "The nations that you have carried away and placed in the cities of Samaria do not know the law of the god of the land; therefore he has sent lions among them; they are killing them, because they do not know the law of the god of the land." Then the king of Assyria commanded, "Send there one of the priests whom you carried away from there; let him go and live there, and teach them the law of the god of the land." So one of the priests whom they had carried away from Samaria came and lived in Bethel; he taught them how they should worship the Lord. But every nation still made gods of its own and put them in the shrines of the high places that the people of Samaria had made, every nation in the cities in which they lived. (2 Kgs 17:24–29)

With this in mind, a few noteworthy points are in order. First, Josephus's words seem to reflect the typical Jewish contempt for those who were both genetically and religiously impure. The xenophobic reinstitution of endogamy initially prescribed by Ezra and Nehemiah (cf. Ezra 10:10, 10:18–44; Neh 13:23–30) after returning from Babylon, had most likely remained an important feature for Josephus and the Jewish community in the midst of later Roman domination. Moreover, though the Cutheans had adopted a form of YHWH worship in order to ward off a "plague of lions," they were still not to be trusted. Likewise, this is also seen in Ezra's account when the "people of the land" said, "We have been sacrificing to him ever since the days of King Esarhaddon of Assyria who brought us here" (Ezra 4:1–2). That is, though the "people of the land" (i.e., likely some mixture containing Israelite Assyrian captives) had come to practice a form of YHWH worship, they were still ultimately rejected and considered to be outside of the covenant community of YHWH by Babylonian returnees. Simply put, they had lost their identity.

Second, as we have seen, Josephus seems to identify the Samaritans with the narrative of 2 Kgs 17. However, the language of 2 Kgs 17 seems to indict the northern tribes also in the multiculturalism and multinationalism that ensued, along with those who worshipped other gods in Samaria: "so they worshiped the Lord but also served their own gods, after the manner of the nations from among whom they had been carried away. To this day they continue to practice their former customs" (2 Kgs 17:33–34). Likewise, according to the context of the biblical narrative, it was the worship of the Canaanite pantheon that had brought about the Assyrian conquest in the first place: "They had worshiped other gods and walked in the customs of the nations" (2 Kgs 17:7–8). Therefore, it is entirely plausible that these "people of the land" were indeed descendants of the amalgamated population of Assyrian vanquished people groups found in 2 Kgs 17. This would have most likely included intermarried Israelite captives.

Thus, in Ezra, it is likely that these were proto-Samaritans, who were likely no longer viewed as purebred Israelites. Instead, they were seen as race-traitors. That is, both their intermarriage (i.e., across ethnic lines) and religious practices were seen as a treasonous act toward those who thought of themselves as a part of the pure covenant community. I, therefore, posit that in the mind of the Babylonian returnees, the Samaritans were seen as descendants of the northern tribes who had integrated with people sent by Assyria from other regions. Likewise, they also realized that those Gentiles who were sent to Samaria soon married both Israelite men and women. Even though these descendants of the northern tribes had retained some form of religious identity, they had still succumbed to the Assyrian populace amalgamation efforts. In the mind of Babylonian returnees, who were seeking to maintain both religious and ethnic purity, this meant that the proto-Samaritans, as well as the northern tribes, were viewed as no different than Gentiles.

Whatever the case, without of some sort of DNA comparison and confirmation, I concede that it is impossible to be 100% certain as to the genetic or biological possibilities of the Samaritans. However, I posit that the data provides us with enough information necessary to make an informed decision their origin. They were no doubt descendants of Assyrian vanquished people groups, which, because of their form of YHWH worship, likely included intermarried Israelites.

I give this topic some space in this study because many have been content with describing the Samaritans as a kind of half-breed. For example, Andreas Köstenberger says: "Samaritans occupied a middle position between Jews and Gentiles, considering themselves Jews but being viewed by Jews as Gentiles."[158] Yet, others have attempted to determine exactly how

---

[158] Andreas J. Köstenberger, *Encountering John: The Gospel in Historical, Literary, and Theological Perspective* (Grand Rapids: Baker Academic, 2013), 87.

much of the northern kingdom's specific cultural practices were retained.[159] However, for the purposes of this study it matters little. Regardless, these groups were viewed as both genetically and religiously impure. Nowhere is this seen more clearly than in John's narrative of Jesus and the Samaritan woman. Whether John's Samaritans were genetically or biologically "fully Gentile" or a "half-breed" matters little. As I have already pointed out, the New Testament writer's (i.e., namely Paul, but also in John) narrative is often a blend of both history and theology. Thus, for the Johannine writer, Israel's Messiah had come to gather these Samaritans—who were viewed as impure by the Jews—into the covenant community of God. That is, the messianic age of Israel's restoration and reconciliation was upon them regardless of their ethnicity. This is akin to what I shall argue in chapter 5: the Gentile nations come to salvation concurrently with the restoration and ingathering of all Israel (i.e., all twelve tribes).

3.5. Summary and Conclusions

What is evident—whether one is a biblical scholar or an archeologist—is that the northern tribes of Israel were indeed conquered by the Assyrians. The conquest and the changes it forced are well attested by the archeological data, Josephus, and the biblical narrative itself. Moreover, this event affected a variety of identity changes for the northern tribes, whether they remained in Samaria or were deported. Here, it must be emphasized that the locations of the deportees—i.e., "Halah, on the Habor, the river of Gozen, and in the cities of the Medes" (2 Kgs 17:6; 18:11)—were

---

[159] Wright, *David*, 144. Wright argues that biblical Israel and historical Israel are not one in the same, and that historical Israel preserved some sense of identity after Assyrian defeat. However, even if this were the case, the biblical narrative is not always concerned with historical exactitude. Instead, its concerns are often theological in nature. Regardless, the northern tribes were probably regarded as both religiously and ethnically impure.

within Assyria and consequently still subject to the effects of conquest.

Therefore, though it is not certain to what extent homogeneous practices remained, what is evident is that the Samarian population—which was once the great capital city of the northern kingdom—eventually, became an eclectic mix of people with no discrete national identity. Moreover, the deportees also suffered a loss of identity to some degree through gradual "Assyrianization," which included changes in language, religious and cultural practices, forced military requirements, and especially an end to the practice of endogamy—as Younger and others suggested.

Thus, Hosea lamenting the northern tribes' perfidy seems to be representing history in explaining that she—as an unfaithful wife—had become a dishonored vessel "swallowed up among the Gentiles nations [MT: הגוים] [LXX: ἔθνεσιν]" (Hos 8:8) and "wanderers among the nations [MT: בגוים] [LXX: ἔθνεσιν]" (Hos 9:17). I will flesh this out more when I discuss Paul's appropriation of the text. Nevertheless, the horror of conquest and exile typically meant the end of a particular ethnic national group. The conquered people would exchange their vanquished gods for the triumphant god of their conquerors. Eventually there would be both cultural and religious assimilation. Moreover, through intermarriage and other forms of multiculturalism, people would vanish as a distinctive entity. I posit that this is exactly what happened to the northern tribes of Israel. It does not matter whether or not there was a total depopulation of Samaria, nor does it matter to what extent religious and cultural practices survived—even in metamorphosed forms. The point of the biblical narrative in Hosea is loss of identity. No doubt, this is something missed by those out searching for an ethnic group. That is, the thrust of the Hosean narrative is that the northern tribes' special status as the covenant people of God was to lose its distinctiveness and be changed to "not my people" (Hos 1:9).

Finally, much speculation—both historical and theological in nature—has evolved over the past two millennia about the precise identity and location of the "ten lost tribes." Where and who are the descendants of the formerly deported Israelites? In my opinion, based on the data available to us, the answer is: *they assimilated into the Gentile nations via the Assyrian conquest and became regarded as Gentiles because of their various losses of distinctive identity*. As we continue in this study, I shall demonstrate that this was indeed likely Paul's view. It is one reason why he is so adamant about not limiting God's new covenant people to race (see Rom 2:25–3:31), while simultaneously maintaining the importance of Israel's covenant promises.

Chapter 4
RETURN FROM EXILE AS A SECOND-TEMPLE PERIOD EXPECTATION

Second-Temple Judaism was not a monolith. That is to say, it was not composed of a single unanimous belief system. Instead, many competing forms of Judaism marked the period. I think most within the guild will agree that it would be incredibly naïve to suggest otherwise. Still yet, a close reading of the literature from the Second-Temple period will reveal that there is a *Leitmotif* of sin (i.e., covenant unfaithfulness), exile (i.e., separation from God's presence), and return from exile (i.e., forgiveness of sins, restoration, new covenant, and a renewed people) throughout its literary corpus. I posit that this *Leitmotif*—i.e., the Second-Temple Jewish expectation for the end of the exile in its diverse forms—is one theme that the apostle Paul (i.e., in Rom 9:25–26) was reworking around his belief that Jesus was Israel's Messiah.

4.1. N.T. Wright and the End of the Exile

Of course, I am not the first to make this suggestion. To date, N.T. Wright has by far made the most influential and yet controversial claims on the Second-Temple period expectation for the end of the exile.[160] In *Jesus and the Victory of God*, Wright's central goal is to shape a new portrait of the historical Jesus. Thus, following Schweitzer, Sanders, and Meyer,[161] Wright posits that

---

[160] For more on this, see Wright, *Climax of the Covenant*; idem, *New Testament and the People of God*; idem, *Jesus and the Victory of God*; idem, *Paul and the Faithfulness of God*.

[161] Sanders, *Jesus and Judaism*; Ben Meyer, *The Aims of Jesus* (London: SCM Press, 1979); Albert Schweitzer, *The Quest of the Historical Jesus: A*

Jesus possessed an apocalyptic messianic self-consciousness whose central mission was to announce the arrival of the kingdom of God and to bring Israel's exile to an end. That is, Jesus believed himself to be "the focal point of the people of YHWH, the returned-from-exile people, the people of the renewed covenant, the people whose sins were now to be forgiven...he came...to bring about the end of exile, the renewal of the covenant, the forgiveness of sins,"[162] which involved "the defeat of evil [Israel's enemies] and the return of YHWH's presence to Zion."[163] In order to substantiate this claim, Wright has set forth the primary thesis that "many, if not most, Jews"[164] of the late Second-Temple period—despite the fact that many had already returned to their homeland from the Babylonian captivity—"regarded the exile as still continuing."[165] That is—as I briefly mentioned in chapter 1— Wright argues that first-century Jews believed the exile to still be in progress, because though a portion of the southern kingdom "had returned in a geographical sense...the great prophecies of restoration had not yet come [completely] true."[166]

Moreover, Wright in his most recent work, *Paul and the Faithfulness of God*, posits that the apostle Paul likewise understood Jesus's mission as centered on the restoration of Israel; and though Paul "freshly revised this belief around Jesus [as Messiah] and the Spirit,"[167] he also shared in the Second-Temple Jewish expectation for the end of the exile. Thus, according to

---

Critical Study of its Progress from Reimarus to Wrede, trans. W. Montgomery (New York: Macmillan, 1968).

[162] Wright, *Jesus and the Victory of God*, 538–39.
[163] *Ibid.*, 477.
[164] Cf. Wright, *Jesus and the People of God*, 268–72; idem, *Jesus and the Victory of God*, 126.
[165] *Ibid.*
[166] *Ibid.*
[167] Wright, *Paul and the Faithfulness of God*, 1049–65.

Wright, Paul believed that the kingdom, the age to come, the new exodus, the end of the exile, the new covenant (i.e., covenant renewal), the new Jerusalem, and the new creation were all inaugurated with Christ's death and resurrection. That is, "the long-awaited expectations of Israel had begun to be realized"[168] in Paul's time. However, in keeping with typical notions of inaugurated eschatology, Wright also suggests that these early Jewish expectations and promises were not consummated during that time. Instead, it was God's divine purpose to create a time lag between realization and consummation, so that the mission to the Gentile nations could advance as Israel's prophets had foretold.[169]

Despite the noteworthy objections of Maurice Casey, who argues that Wright's arguments and evidence on the matter are "quite spurious,"[170] I think Wright is generally on the correct path. Indeed, the themes of exile and restoration are crucial components for a correct understanding of early "Jewish Restoration Eschatology."[171] However, my major contention is with Wright's lack of attention given toward the northern tribes and the Assyrian exile. I concur with Wright that the Second-Temple literature supports the theory of an ongoing exile, but I suggest—as does Pitre[172]—that this is not because of Roman political domination. Instead, it is due to a concern for the whereabouts of the Assyrian exiles. The fact is that not "all Israel" had returned in a

---

[168] *Ibid.*, 1078.

[169] It is interesting that Wright never comments on the expected length of time lag between realization and consummation. That is, he never really works out a futurist eschatology. In other words, he never states what he might think is the expected length or consummation of the mission to the Gentiles. As I see it, this leaves much room for one to only speculate about his eschatology.

[170] Maurice Casey, "Where Wright Is Wrong: A Critical Review of N. T. Wright's *Jesus and the Victory of God*," *JSNT* 69 (1998): 95–103.

[171] Sanders is to be credited for this phrase—see *Jesus and Judaism*, 87.

[172] Pitre, *Jesus, the Tribulation, and the End of the Exile*, 31–40.

geographical sense.¹⁷³ The great prophecies of restoration that Wright suggests had not yet come completely true—as we shall see—also involved the northern tribes. Thus, I posit that there is enough evidence to suggest that both Israel's prophets and Second-Temple Jews were also looking for the return of the northern tribes (i.e., Israel). That is, much of the literature of the period seems to assume that as long as parts of Israel's twelve tribes remained scattered, then the promise of return from exile remained unfulfilled.

Therefore, in this chapter, I examine both Israel's Scriptures and the Second-Temple period literature for instances of the expectation of return from exile, along with traces of just how the northern tribes might have fit into their thought in this period. I should note that for the purposes of this study, I am required to be somewhat ephemeral. I do not have the space to review all evidence that might exist. Additionally, I do not wish to be repetitious of what others have already pointed out.¹⁷⁴ Thus, what follows is only a brief examination of some of the most significant evidence for the purposes of this study. Nevertheless, I think this section will show that the return from exile was indeed a Second-Temple expectation, yet one that also involved the return of the northern tribes. This understanding will then provide the needed support for the suggestion that Paul's reworking of this anticipation was also inclusive of the northern tribes.

---

¹⁷³ By "all Israel," I do not mean every individual member, nor do I mean "only Judah." Instead, as I argue in chapter 5, it is a term that also extends to the divorced northern tribes.

¹⁷⁴ Pitre and Evans have both illustrated instances of the return-from-exile motif in Second-Temple literature—see Pitre, *Jesus, the Tribulation, and the End of the Exile*, 41–127; Craig A. Evans, "Jesus and the Continuing Exile of Israel," in *Jesus and The Restoration of Israel: A Critical Assessment of N. T. Wright's Jesus and the Victory of God*, ed. Carey C. Newman (Downers Grove, IL: InterVarsity, 1999), 77–100.

4.2. Israel's Scriptures

The Second-Temple period has a proper literary underpinning. No doubt certain Jews of this period found in the words of their prophets, the source with which to expect the fulfillment of both messianic and eschatological hopes. That is, the image found in the Jewish literature of this period was deeply drawn upon from Israel's Scriptures. A close look at these particular Scriptures reveals that, though the prophets repeatedly rebuked Israel for her sins, they also promised her restoration in the future. This restoration was coterminous with the promised end of exile, which always anticipated the return of *both* houses of Israel (i.e., all twelve tribes of Israel).

4.2.1. Isaiah

I begin with the prophet who is undoubtedly foundational to the majority of Paul's claims: Isaiah.[175] Significant to our study is the fact that the prophet unquestionably has both houses of Israel in mind when he speaks of the ingathering of Israel's exiles from the four corners of the earth:

> On that day the root of Jesse shall stand as a signal to the peoples; the nations shall inquire of him, and his dwelling shall be glorious. On that day the Lord will extend his hand yet a second time to recover the remnant that is left of his people, from Assyria, from Egypt, from Pathros, from Ethiopia, from Elam, from Shinar, from Hamath, and from the coastlands of the sea. He will raise a signal for the nations, and will assemble the *outcasts of [the house of] Israel* and gather the *dispersed of Judah* from the four corners of the earth. The jealousy of *Ephraim* shall depart,

---

[175] For an extensive survey of Paul's use of Isaiah in Romans, see Wagner, *Heralds*.

> the hostility of *Judah* shall be cut off; Ephraim shall not be jealous of Judah, and Judah shall not be hostile towards Ephraim. (Isa 11:10–13—emphasis added)

The context clearly suggests that my addition, "the house of," is warranted (cf. Isa 10:24). It is Assyria who is used as a rod of God's anger to punish Israel for her sins (cf. Isa 10:5–19). However, "on that day," the Assyrian yoke will be removed and God's "indignation will come to an end" (Isa 10:24–25). Moreover, both Ephraim and Judah will be reunited, and jointly, they "will plunder the people of the east" (Isa 11:13–14), and "there shall be a highway from Assyria" (Isa 11:16). Therefore, we can reasonably conclude that Isa 11:11 refers not only to the return of Judah but also the ingathering of Israel's exiles from Assyria— i.e., the northern tribes.

At this point in our study—though I will provide a deeper analysis in chapter 5—I would be remiss if I did not mention now one most notable point of connection between Paul and Isaiah. Significant to our study is the fact that coterminous with the gathering of the outcasts of Israel and the dispersed of Judah, is the time when the Gentiles shall put their hope in "the root of Jesse." In Rom 15:12, Paul quotes Isa 11:10 verbatim (i.e., with the LXX) as a messianic reference. It is the ἡ ῥίζα τοῦ Ἰεσσαί—the one ἀνιστάμενος ἄρχειν ἐθνῶν—in whom the Gentiles will hope (Rom 15:12 // Isa 11:10 LXX: ἡ ῥίζα τοῦ Ιεσσαι καὶ ὁ ἀνιστάμενος ἄρχειν ἐθνῶν ἐπ'αὐτῷ ἔθνη ἐλπιοῦσιν). Of course, Isaiah's broader context has to do with the eschatological restoration and ingathering of Israel from exile. However, in Rom 15, Paul ties the verse to the inclusion of Gentiles, which comes as a result of the work of the Messiah. Thus, for Paul, the gathering of Israel's exiles and the salvation of the Gentile nations are coterminous events.

Commentators seem to agree on the previous point.[176] However, none draw in the nuanced connection of the Assyrian captives. For example, Dunn says: "Isaiah's vision of the Messiah's rule embracing the nations (Gentiles) and of Gentiles finding their hope in him (Isa 11:10) would now, finally, be realized (Rom 15:12)."[177] Moreover, as Wagner states: "[Isaiah 11:10] envisions the restoration of Israel issuing in blessing for Gentiles and for the entire created order."[178] Additionally, Schreiner interprets Paul's quotation to mean "harmony will exist between Jews and Gentiles when both groups hope in the shoot of Jesse."[179] Likewise, Keener does not seem to make a proper distinction between the northern tribes and Jews, instead: "[In Rom 15] the Messiah would bring salvation and the knowledge of God to all nations...and would likewise precipitate the restoration of the scattered Jewish people."[180] Though these suggestions are all correct, the context is equally clear that this time also involves a gathering of the Assyrian exiles. Thus, while I agree with these conclusions, I also suggest that Paul had in mind those northern tribes who were "scattered" among the Gentile nations by Assyria (Hos 7:8; 8:8). It is precisely at this point that the method mentioned in chapter 2 comes into play—i.e., narrative intertextuality. The broader context of Paul's quotation of Isaiah suggests that he is recalling Israel's entire narrative and not just

---

[176] Cranfield, *Romans*, 2:747; Douglas Moo, *Romans*, NICNT (Grand Rapids: Eerdmans, 1996), 319; Craig Keener, *Romans*, NCCS (Cambridge: Lutterworth Press, 2009), 173; Thomas R. Schreiner, *Romans*, BECNT (Grand Rapids: Baker Academic, 1998), 759; James D. G. Dunn, *Romans 1-8*, WBC 34A (Dallas: Word, 1988), 133-36, 847.

[177] James D. G. Dunn, *Jesus, Paul, and the Gospels* (Grand Rapids: Eerdmans, 2011), 161.

[178] Wagner, *Heralds*, 318.

[179] Schreiner, *Romans*, 759.

[180] Keener, *Romans*, 173.

selective parts. If so, then Paul's mission to the Gentiles is also inclusive of the northern tribes. Moreover, by his Jew and Gentile reconciliation program, as seen by his use of Isa 11 in Rom 15:12, Paul likely believed that he was witnessing the literal jealousy of Ephraim departing and the hostility of Judah being cut off (cf. Isa 11:10–13).

4.2.2. Jeremiah

Jeremiah suggests that at the time when "all nations shall gather…to the presence of the Lord in Jerusalem…the house of Judah shall join the house of Israel and together they shall come from the land of the north to the land that I gave your ancestors for a heritage" (Jer 3:17–18). Moreover, of Ephraim it is said: "I am going to bring them from the land of the north and gather them from the farthest parts of the earth" (Jer 31:8). Clearly, Jeremiah posits that as Ephraim is restored, so it will be for all Israel:

> "For the days are surely coming," says the Lord, "when I will restore the fortunes of my people, *Israel* and *Judah*, says the Lord, and I will bring them back to the land that I gave to their ancestors and the shall take possession of it. These are the words that the Lord spoke concerning Israel and Judah." (Jer 30:3–4—emphasis added)

Moreover, at the time when God restores "the fortunes of [his] people, Israel and Judah," and when God "brings them back to the land…they shall be called my people" (Jer 30:3–4, 22). The fact that both Israel and Judah are called "my people" is significant in light of Hosea's declaration that the northern kingdom is "not my people" (Hos 1:9), a declaration certainly known to both Jeremiah (Jer 3:8) and to Paul (Rom 9:25–26). Furthermore, this restoration is one and the same with the time of the Righteous Branch:

"The days are coming," says the Lord, "when I will raise up for David a righteous Branch, and he shall execute justice and righteousness in the land. In the days *Judah* will be saved and *Israel* will live in safety. And this is the name by which he will be called: 'The Lord is our righteousness.' Therefore, the days are surely coming," says the Lord, "when it shall no longer be said, 'As the Lord lives who brought the people of Israel out of the land of the north and out of all the lands where he had driven them.' Then they shall live in their own land." (Jer 23:5–8—emphasis added)

No doubt, the Davidic lineage is a staple of Paul's messianic mindset. Thus, it should be noted that though the LXX attaches the article ταῖς to the dative feminine plural noun ἡμέραις—thus rendering verse 6 as "ἐν ταῖς ἡμέραις" (i.e., in the days)—the MT uses the term, בימיו (i.e., in his days). For whatever reason, the commentators have failed to point this out, as I have found no discussion to-date. Nevertheless, as we have seen elsewhere (e.g., Isa 11; Rom 15), this proves significant for the Christological dimensions of Paul's exilic-return motif. That is, Paul perennially interprets Israel's return-from-exile in light of his belief in Jesus as Israel's Messiah, and therefore ties it around that event. Likewise, for Jeremiah, the transitions of both Israel and Judah back to "my people" are coterminous events with the time when all nations shall gather to the presence of the Lord in Jerusalem around the raising of the Davidic king, which for Paul is Jesus, who is Israel's Messiah.

One further observation is in order. Jeremiah undoubtedly has both houses of Israel in mind when he speaks of the future establishment of the new covenant:

"The days are surely coming," says the Lord, "when I will make a new covenant with the house of Israel and the house of Judah. It will not be like the covenant that I made with their ancestors when I took them by the hand to bring them out of the land of Egypt—a covenant that they broke, though I was their husband," says the Lord. "But this is the covenant that I will make with the house of Israel after those days," says the Lord, "I will put my law within them, and I will write it on their hearts; and I will be their God, and they shall be my people. No longer shall they teach one another, or say to each other, 'Know the Lord,' for they shall all know me, from the least of them to the greatest," says the Lord, "for I will forgive their iniquity, and remember their sin no more." (Jer 31:31–34)

Throughout his epistles, Paul uses "new covenant" terminology (e.g., Rom 9, 11; 2 Cor 3; Gal 3, 4; cf. Eph 2). In particular, and as can be seen from the figure below, I suggest that Paul strongly echoes Jer 31:34 in Rom 11:27:

Figure 4.1: Jer 31:34 in Rom 11:27

Jer 31:34 LXX	Rom 11:27
καὶ **τῶν ἁμαρτιῶν αὐτῶν** οὐ μὴ μνησθῶ ἔτι	καὶ αὕτη αὐτοῖς ἡ παρ' ἐμοῦ διαθήκη, ὅταν ἀφέλωμαι **τὰς ἁμαρτίας αὐτῶν**.

The volume, availability, thematic coherence, and historical plausibility of this echo are strong enough to suggest that Paul here echoes the prophet in order to indicate that his own mission to the Gentiles is the fulfillment of Jeremiah's new covenant.[181] For Paul,

---

[181] This echo meets the following criteria: Availability: Paul undoubtedly has access to Jeremiah; Volume: synonymous phrases such as τῶν ἁμαρτιῶν

God is undoubtedly placing his law in his people and writing it on their hearts (i.e., Rom 2, 7; 2 Cor 3:1–3). Of course, what I am suggesting is certainly not new, as it is the frequent suggestion of commentators that Paul speaks of Jeremiah's new covenant in Rom 11:27.[182] However, I have yet to uncover their mention of the significance of the northern tribes. For the prophet, the forgiving and forgetting of Israel's iniquity would be the fulfillment of the new covenant. It is at this time that both the house of Israel and the house of Judah will be restored. Moreover, as I suggested above, the larger context of Jer 31 says that Ephraim shall return from among the nations (cf. Jer 31:1–22). By echoing this passage, Paul posits the fulfillment of the new covenant. Yet, if our argument holds true, the fulfillment of the new covenant also demands the return of the northern tribes from exile.

4.2.3. Ezekiel

Ezekiel explains how God shall reunite both Judah and Ephraim. Here, once again, the restoration of all twelve tribes of Israel is clearly in view:

> Thus says the Lord God: I am about to take the *stick of Joseph (which is in the hand of Ephraim) and the tribes of Israel* associated with it; and I will put the *stick of Judah* upon it, and *make them one stick*, in order that they may be *one in my hand*. When the sticks on which you write are in your hand before their eyes, then say to them, thus says the

---

αὐτῶν and τὰς ἁμαρτίας αὐτῶν (the sins of them); Thematic Coherence: Paul perennially uses "new covenant" terminology elsewhere; Historical Plausibility: Paul's readers were undoubtedly familiar with and expectant of Jeremiah's new covenant, knowing it meant the forgetting of sin.

[182] Joseph A. Fitzmyer, *Romans: A New Translation with Introduction and Commentary*, AB 33 (New York: Doubleday, 1993), 625; Robert Jewett, *Romans: A Commentary* (Minneapolis: Fortress, 2007), 704–705.

> Lord God: *I will take the people of Israel from the nations among which they have gone, and will gather them from every quarter, and bring them to their own land.* I will make them one nation in the land, on the mountains of Israel; and one king shall be king over them all. *Never again shall they be two nations, and never again shall they be divided into two kingdoms.* (Ezek 37:19–22—emphasis added)

For Ezekiel, the exile ends when both kingdoms become "one stick," as he posited, the Lord "will take the people of Israel from the nations among which they have gone…[and] never again shall they be two nations, and never again shall they be divided into two kingdoms" (Ezek 37:21–22).

Additionally, Ezekiel's vision imagined that this would all happen under a Davidic King: "My servant David shall be king over them; and they shall all have one Shepherd" (Ezek 37:24). Furthermore, Ezekiel's vision imagined that this would be at the time of the establishment of the new covenant: "I will make a covenant of peace with them; it shall be an everlasting covenant with them; and I will bless them and multiply them, and will set my sanctuary among them forevermore" (Ezek 37:26). Finally, all of this would happen by God's Spirit—an obvious sign of salvific regeneration and restoration, "I will put my spirit within you, and you shall live, and I will place you on your own soil; then you shall know that I, the Lord, have spoken and will act, says the Lord" (Ezek 37:14).

Of course, I have already argued for Paul's use of new covenant terminology in the previous section. Moreover, commentators have demonstrated that Ezek 37 is present elsewhere in Paul.[183] Ezek 37–39 speaks of the return and restoration of all twelve tribes from exile.[184] Contemporaneous with this event are both the coming of the Messiah (Ezek 37:15–28) and the conversion of the Gentile nations (Ezek 37:28). Equally, the Gentile nations are converted as Israel is restored from exile (Ezek 39:21–29). Thus, we can determine that these are all coterminous events.

4.2.4. Daniel

Though both Hebrew and Aramaic portions of Daniel indicate characteristics of a late period of development, I have decided to include it among my evaluation of Hebrew Bible exilic literature.[185] However, it should be noted that much of the book

---

[183] Cf. Dunn, *Romans 1–8*, 429; Tom Holland, *Romans: The Divine Marriage: A Biblical Theological Commentary* (Eugene, OR: Wipf and Stock, 2011), 184. They both demonstrate Paul's use of Ezek 37 in 1 Cor 15.

[184] Scholars have routinely pointed out that Ezek 37 and the themes of exile and the restoration of Israel are contiguous with the resurrection of the dead. Jon Levenson has argued that Ezek 37 is about "both the national restoration of Israel and the later resurrection of a flesh" (*Resurrection and the Restoration of Israel the Ultimate Victory of the God of Life* [New Haven: Yale University Press, 2006] 156–80). He spends much of his book challenging what has been the consensus of critical scholarship that future resurrection of the flesh is a late development within Judaism. Moreover, Pitre has argued, "this connection between resurrection and restoration finds its classic expression in Ezekiel's vision of the valley of dry bones, whose bodily resurrection signals the ingathering of the twelve tribes of Israel, the coming of the Davidic Messiah, and the End of the Exile" (Pitre, *Jesus, the Tribulation, and the End of the Exile*, 414).

[185] "The Hebrew of Daniel has little in common with the exilic period. Rather, it falls in the range of Second Temple Hebrew." Moreover, "between 167 and 164 BCE the Hebrew chapters 8–12 were added, and chapter 1 [most likely, but not necessarily] was translated to provide a Hebrew frame for the Aramaic chapters. The glosses in 12:11–12 were added before the rededication of the temple. Additionally, the Aramaic of Daniel sometimes shares some

likely falls into the category of late Second-Temple literature. Moreover, within the guild, there is a near consensus among Hebrew Bible scholars that chapters 7–12 should be read as a pseudepigraphic addition from the Seleucid Period.[186] The point is, regardless of when the book was written, it still adds weight to my argument. In fact, even more so, the later it was written.

If the writer of Daniel is indeed from the Seleucid period, then the fact that he undoubtedly has Jeremiah in mind when he says, "according to the word of the Lord to the prophet Jeremiah" (Dan 9:2) speaks to the mindset of Jews during this period. That is, the prayer of the writer from this period echoes Jeremiah and shares his concern for the future restoration of both houses of Israel:

> Righteousness is on your side, O Lord, but open shame, as at this day, falls on us, the people of *Judah, the inhabitants of Jerusalem*, and *all Israel, those who are near and those who are far away*, in all the lands to which you have driven them, because of the treachery that they have committed against you. (Dan 9:7—emphasis added)

As I have already demonstrated, Jeremiah's gathering of exiles included both houses of Israel. Here, the writer of Daniel adopts

---

affinities with the Aramaic forms found in "texts from the Dead Sea," which means these have a final redactionary form that belongs to the Maccabean period—see John J. Collins, *Daniel: A Commentary on the Book of Daniel*, with Adela Yarbro Collins; ed. Frank Moore Cross (Minneapolis: Fortress, 1993), 20. See also, Frank M. Cross, "Discovery of the Samaria Papyri," *BA* 26.4 (1963): 110–21.

[186] The consensus among Hebrew Bible/Old Testament scholars is numerous. To name but a few: see S. R. Driver, *An Introduction to the Literature of the Old Testament* (New York: Meridian Books, 1956); Collins, *Daniel*, 1993; Anathea Portier-Young, "Languages of Identity and Obligation: Daniel as Bilingual Book," *VT* 60.1 (2010): 98–115.

Jeremiah's theme of return-from-exile by use of the phrase "lands where he had driven them" (Jer 16:15; 23:3). Thus, the writer of Daniel also likely posits the return of both houses of Israel.

Concerning Paul's possible use of Daniel, few scholars have written on it.[187] However, I suggest that Dan 9 was likely deep in the recesses of Paul's mind. For example, Jer 31:34, Dan 9:24, and Rom 11:27 all posit the taking away of Israel's sin at the time of a Davidic King (i.e., anoint the most holy), and at the time of the new covenant (Dan 9:27). Thus, we can determine that these are all coterminous events.

4.2.5. Hosea

According to the Hosean writer, both "the *people of Judah* and the *people of Israel* shall be gathered together, and they shall appoint for themselves one head; and they shall take possession of the land, for great shall be the day of Jezreel" (Hos 1:11—emphasis added). No doubt, this is a picture of God's purpose to overcome Israel's unfaithfulness, to restore her to himself, and to end the exile at an unspecified point in the future. Nevertheless, for Hosea, this restoration clearly anticipated the return of both houses of Israel.

Moreover, it is noteworthy to mention that the gathering of both Israel and Judah would be at the time they "appoint one head." Though it is not explicit here, Hosea makes it clear elsewhere that this is an obvious reference to a restored Davidic rule: "Afterward the Israelites shall return and seek the Lord their God, and David their king; they shall come in awe to the Lord and

---

[187] Craig A. Evans, "Daniel in the New Testament: Visions of God's Kingdom" in *The Book of Daniel: Composition and Reception*, vol. 2; eds. J. J. Collins and P. W. Flint (Leiden: Brill, 2001), 523–25. This is the only discussion I have found to date. Evans discussed the possible influence of Daniel in 1 Cor 15.

to his goodness in the latter days" (Hos 3:5). Thus, for Hosea, the gathering of exiles—which involved both houses of Israel—is contemporaneous with the rule of the Davidic King. This is most significant in light of the fact that Paul interprets the return from exile in light of his belief in Jesus as Israel's Messiah. I shall say more on Hosea in chapter 5.

4.3. Apocrypha/Pseudepigrapha
4.3.1. Tobit

Among Second-Temple Jewish pseudepigraphal writings, the first witness to the expectation of return from exile is found in the book of Tobit. The consensus is that the author of Tobit is writing between 225 and 175 BCE.[188] Moreover, the Qumran copies of Tobit (4Q196–200) date from 100 BCE to 25 CE—the Hebrew fragment 4Q200 being the latest (30 BCE–25 CE).[189] This suggests that, though the book obviously was not composed during this later period, the narrative itself was still experiencing a certain level of popularity and was in circulation possibly into the first century.

Tobit's character is that of a devoutly religious man from one of the tribes of Israel (i.e., Naphtali), who continually emphasizes his own righteousness over and against the decision of his own people (i.e., other members of the northern tribes) to mingle with the Gentiles and their customs (cf. Tob 1:10–12). Tobit's desire is for his son to follow endogamous restrictions in marriage (4:12–13). Moreover, his character exhibits a particular nationalistic behavior (5:9–14), which has an interest in preserving identity in the midst of exile. These examples provide us with an understanding of the general mindset of some during the Second-

---

[188] See Joseph A. Fitzmyer, *Tobit* (Berlin: Walter De Gruyter, 2003), 3–58; Geza Vermes, ed., *The Complete Dead Sea Scrolls in English* (London: Penguin, 2011), 594–601.

[189] Vermes, *Dead Sea Scrolls*, 594.

Temple period. That is, several still thought Israelite identity was at stake or had been frustrated on some level, because the writer understands that many Israelites had married foreign women while in exile (see 1:9; 4:12).

However, more important to our study is the fact that the writer has an enduring concern for those who had been "dispersed...among all the nations" (Tob 3:4) or those "scattered...among...the nations" (Tob 13:3). In fact, a central theme in the narrative has to do with the expectation of return from exile of *all* Israel. That is, all those who were taken as captives from both Samaria and Jerusalem:

> For I know and believe that whatever God has said will be fulfilled and will come true; not a single word of the prophecies will fail. All of our kindred, inhabitants of the land of Israel, will be *scattered* and taken as captives from the good land; and the whole land of Israel will be desolate, even *Samaria* and *Jerusalem* will be desolate. And the temple of God in it will be burned to the ground, and it will be desolate for a while. But God will again have mercy on them, and God will bring *them* back into the land of Israel; and they will rebuild the temple of God, but not like the first one until the period when the times of fulfillment shall come. After this they all will return from their exile and will rebuild Jerusalem in splendor; and in it the temple of God will be rebuilt, just as the prophets of Israel have said concerning it. Then the nations in the whole world will all be converted and worship God in truth. They will all abandon their idols, which deceitfully have led them into their error; and in righteousness they will praise the eternal God. All the *Israelites who are saved in those days and are truly mindful of God will be gathered together*; they will go

to Jerusalem and live in safety forever in the land of Abraham, and it will be given over to them. Those who sincerely love God will rejoice, but those who commit sin and injustice will vanish from all the earth. (Tob 14:4–7—emphasis added)[190]

It should be noted that the writer of Tobit's narrative could also be seen as analogous to the story of Israel. That is, Tobit's condition is paradigmatic for the exiled northern tribes. Of this, Richard Bauckham has pointed out: "Tobit's story is a parable of Israel's story from exile to restoration…Tobit's eschatological prospect is not simply the restoration of the exiles of Judah, but…the return of the exiles of the northern tribes to the land and their reconciliation to Jerusalem, as the national and cultic centre."[191] Craig Evans agrees saying, "Tobit in various ways speaks of Israel's continuing exile and…foresees the day when the scattered tribes will be regathered."[192]

Nonetheless, just as God has punished Tobit, so he has also done with Israel by causing them to suffer the horror of exile. However, God's restoration soon comes to Tobit and his family along with the promise that the Israelites will also soon be restored into their land: "He will gather you from all the nations among whom you have been scattered" (Tob 13:5b). That is, the narrative tells of the misfortunes of a man and his family in exile. These calamities are ultimately restored as demons are cast out (Tob 8:1–3), the blind receive their sight (Tob 11:14), and poverty turns to

---

[190] Citations of Tobit and 1–2 Maccabees are taken from *The New Oxford Annotated Apocrypha: NRSV*, ed. Michael D. Coogan (New York: Oxford University Press, 2010).

[191] Richard Bauckham, *The Jewish World Around the New Testament*, WUNT 1/233 (Tübingen: Mohr Siebeck, 2008), 434.

[192] Evans, "Jesus and the Continuing Exile of Israel," 87.

wealth (Tob 2:11; 12:1–5). Thus, God's deliverance through the angelic messenger Raphael brings about the hope for restoration from the exile. Thus, the expectation of restoration and return from exile in the final chapters (Tob 13–14) form an *inclusio* with chapter one (Tob 1:1–3, 10) in that they are both speaking of Israel in exile. It should be noted however that Tobit seems to be strangely silent about any messianic hopes tied with the eschaton.

4.3.2. The Wisdom of Ben Sira

The Wisdom of Ben Sira was likely composed in Jerusalem sometime between 196–175 BCE.[193] Originally written in Hebrew, it was later translated into Greek in Egypt.[194] In this book, the writer expresses his future hope for Israel's restoration return from exile in three different places: Sir 36:1–16, 48:10, and 51:12. Here, the return-from-exile motif seems to be largely articulated in comparison to a much wider argument of Israel's significance in the Hellenistic world. This seems to indicate that the book was probably composed around the time that Seleucus was succeeded by Antiochus IV.

In Sir 36:1–16, an indication of concern for Israel's ultimate vindication, restoration, and ingathering is found. Whether or not these verses are a later interpolation matters very little,[195] as they still lend support to the expectation of return-from-exile in the Second-Temple period. The writer contends:

---

[193] George W.E. Nickelsburg, *Jewish Literature Between the Bible and the Mishnah: A Historical and Literary Introduction* (Minneapolis: Fortress, 2005), 62.

[194] *Ibid.*, 53.

[195] Collins argues that it is a later Maccabean interpolation—see *Jewish Wisdom in the Hellenistic Age* (Louisville: Westminster John Knox Press, 1997), 109–11. Regardless, this still adds weight to my argument.

> Have mercy upon us, O God of all, and put all the nations in fear of you. Lift up your hand against foreign nations and let them see your might. As you have used us to show your holiness to them, so use them to show your glory to us. Then they will know, as we have known, that there is no God but you, O Lord. Give *new signs*, and work *other wonders*; make your *hand* and *right arm* glorious. Rouse your anger and pour out your wrath; destroy the adversary and wipe out the enemy. Hasten the day, and remember the appointed time, and let people recount your mighty deeds. Let survivors be consumed in the fiery wrath, and may those who harm your people meet destruction. Crush the heads of hostile rulers who say, "There is no one but ourselves." Gather *all* the tribes of Jacob, and give them their inheritance, as at the beginning. (Sir 36:1–16—emphasis added)

What is the mention of *new* signs, hand, *other* wonders, and right arm, but an allusion to the Exodus (Exod 11:9–10; 15:6; Deut 4:34)? As Evans points out, "The signs and wonders for which Ben Sira longed are those God performed in liberating Israel from Egypt, protecting Israel in the wilderness and enabling Israel to take possession of the promise land."[196] Moreover, the *new* or *other* point to a type of second exodus, which clearly involves the gathering of all twelve tribes of Jacob.[197]

---

[196] Evans, "Jesus and the Continuing Exile of Israel," 82.

[197] Throughout this study, I use the terminology of "end of the exile," "restoration of Israel," and "new exodus" somewhat generally to refer to the same event. That is, the ingathering of the scattered tribes of Israel from among the Gentiles. For a more nuanced definition of these terms see Pitre, *Jesus, the Tribulation, and the End of the Exile*, 31–40.

Additionally, the writer's appropriation of Mal 4:5–6 deserves our attention. In addition to turning "the hearts of parents to their children and the hearts of children to their parents," Elijah as the restorer of Israel will return "at the appointed time...to calm the wrath of God before it breaks out in fury...and to restore the tribes of Jacob" (Sir 48:10). Here we can see that Elijah's role is expanded to include nationalistic restorer, which for Ben Sira, is still a future expectation.

Finally, found only in the Hebrew text is a series of praises given in Ben Sira's prayer. The most notable for our purposes is the mention of "him who gathers the dispersed of Israel" (Sir 51:12). This praise is recited here as a statement to the present Second-Temple circumstances. That is, those living in Jerusalem in Ben Sira's time should still expect the ingathering of the dispersed.

4.3.3. *The Book of Jubilees*

The book of Jubilees is a narrative recasting of the biblical account from Gen 1 to Exod 12. It dates sometime between 168–100 BCE.[198] The author not only recasts Israel's prehistory, but expresses the future hope for Israel's restoration and return from exile:

> And I will hide my face from them, and I will deliver them into the hand of the Gentiles for captivity, and for a prey, and for devouring, and I will remove them from the midst of the land, and *I will scatter them amongst the Gentiles*. And they will forget all my law and all my commandments and all my judgments, and will go astray as to new moons, and Sabbaths, and festivals, and jubilees, and ordinances. And after this they will turn to me from amongst the Gentiles with all their heart and with all their soul and with

---

[198] Nickelsburg, *Jewish Literature Between the Bible and the Mishnah*, 73.

> all their strength, and *I will gather them from amongst all the Gentiles*, and they will seek me, so that I shall be found of them, when they seek me with all their heart and with all their soul. (*Jub.* 1:12–14—emphasis added)[199]

Most striking for the purposes of our study are the writer's echoes of Jer 31 and Hos 1, which I have already shown to have both houses of Israel in mind. That is, the writer of Jubilees uses both Jeremiah's and Hosea's language to support his claims of future restoration:

> And after this they will turn to me in all uprightness and with all (their) heart and with all (their) soul, and *I will circumcise the foreskin of their heart and the foreskin of the heart of their seed, and I will create in them a holy spirit*, and I will cleanse them so that they shall not turn away from me from that day unto eternity. And their souls will cleave to me and to all my commandments, and they will fulfill my commandments, and I will be their Father and they shall be my children. And they all *shall be called children of the living God*, and every angel and every spirit shall know, yea, they shall know that these are my children, and that I am their Father in uprightness and righteousness, and that I love them. And do you write down for yourself all these words which I declare unto you on this mountain, the first and the last, which will come to pass in all the divisions of the days in the law and in the testimony and in the weeks and the jubilees unto eternity, until I descend and

---

[199] Translations of the book of Jubilees are taken from *The Apocrypha and Pseudepigrapha of the Old Testament in English*, ed. R.H. Charles; 2 vols. (Oxford: Clarendon Press, 1913).

dwell with them throughout eternity. (*Jub.* 1:22–25—emphasis added)

The significance of this observation cannot be ignored. The writer's interpretive strategy for Israel's restoration is analogous with both Hosea and Jeremiah, who saw the future restoration and return from exile—at the time of the new covenant—as involving both the house of Israel and the house of Judah. Once again:

"The days are surely coming," says the Lord, "when *I will make a new covenant with the house of Israel and the house of Judah*. It will not be like the covenant that I made with their ancestors when I took them by the hand to bring them out of the land of Egypt—a covenant that they broke, though I was their husband," says the Lord. "But this is the covenant that I will make with the house of Israel after those days, says the Lord: *I will put my law within them, and I will write it on their hearts; and I will be their God, and they shall be my people.*" (Jer 31:31–33—emphasis added)

Yet the number of the people of Israel shall be like the sand of the sea, which can be neither measured nor numbered; and in the place where it was said to them, "You are not my people," it shall be said to them, "*Children of the living God*." *The people of Judah and the people of Israel shall be gathered together*, and they shall appoint for themselves one head; and they shall take possession of the land, for great shall be the day of Jezreel. (Hos 1:10–11—emphasis added)

The weight of this observation for understanding Paul's interpretive strategy in Romans will become obvious as we progress into chapter 5. However, for now it will suffice to say that like the writer of Jubilees, Paul echoes the phrase: "they shall be called children of the living God" (Rom 9:26). Likewise, he uses both Jeremiah's and Hosea's language to support his claims of the future restoration of all Israel.

4.3.4. Second Maccabees

Second Maccabees is an abridgment of a five-volume history of Israel during the years 180–161 BCE.[200] Jason of Cyrene ostensibly composed the initial history sometime after 161 BCE (cf. 2 Macc 2:19–32).[201] Second Maccabees has been prefixed with two separate letters (2 Macc 1:1–9; 1:10–2:18), which are both considered to be later interpolations—with 1:1–9 likely dating to 125–124 BCE, and 1:10–2:18 to 100 BCE.[202]

Evans has rightly concluded that the writer of the prefixed second letter believed the exile was still in progress, pointing out that the location of the "tent and the ark and alter of incense" (2 Macc 2:5) will "remain unknown until God gathers his people together again" (2 Macc 2:7).[203] The writer of the second letter then places the locus of 2 Maccabees' meaning within the themes of exile and restoration: "As he promised through the law, we have hope in God that he will soon have mercy on us and *will gather us from everywhere* under heaven into his holy place, for he has

---

[200] *Ibid.*, 1:106.

[201] Daniel J. Harrington, *Invitation to the Apocrypha* (Grand Rapids: Eerdmans, 1999), 137–51.

[202] Jonathan Goldstein, *II Maccabees*, AB 41A (New York: Doubleday, 1983), 24–27.

[203] Evans, "Jesus and the Continuing Exile of Israel," 83.

rescued us from great evils and has purified the place" (2 Macc 2:18).

Here, the writer sees the emancipation of Jerusalem and its temple (2 Macc 10:1–9) by Judas Maccabeus as a forerunner to Israel's return from exile. That is, along with the idea of restoration, there exists a return-from-exile motif. For example, "it is God who has saved all his people, and has returned the inheritance to all, and the kingship and the priesthood and the consecration" (2 Macc 2:17). Likewise, God "will [still] soon have mercy on us and will gather us from everywhere under heaven into his holy place" (2 Macc 2:18). These suggest that the return from exile is still the future expectation of the writer after the liberation of Jerusalem and its temple. That is, the writer assumes a sort of collective yet unfinished expectation that God "will [still] gather *us* from everywhere" (2 Macc 2:17–18). In other words, as long as parts of Israel remained scattered—regardless of those Jews currently inhabiting Jerusalem—then the promise of return from exile remained unfulfilled.

4.3.5. The Psalms of Solomon

Originally in Hebrew, the Psalms of Solomon was likely composed between 63–30 BCE in Jerusalem.[204] It reflects the feelings of devout Jews living in Jerusalem in the first century BCE. In their view, the current troubles are God's discipline for breaking the covenant. Thus, the writer shares solidarity with his community in hoping for the future restoration of Israel, which will begin when the Davidic King comes to restore the true worship of YHWH and establish the kingdom of God. Moreover, when he comes, he will gather those scattered (*Pss. Sol.* 17:31). As a result,

---

[204] Nickelsburg, *Jewish Literature Between the Bible and the Mishnah*, 246–47.

the Gentile nations will come and worship the king in Jerusalem. Specifically, the writer declares:

> *He will gather a holy people* whom he will lead in righteousness; and he will judge the tribes of the people that have been made holy by the Lord their God. He will not tolerate unrighteousness (even) to pause among them, and any person who knows wickedness shall not live with them. For he shall know them that they are all children of their God. He will distribute them upon the land according to their tribes; the alien and the foreigner will no longer live near them. He will judge people and nations in the wisdom of his righteousness. *And he will have Gentile nations serving him under his yoke,* and he will glorify the Lord in (a place) prominent (above) the whole earth. And he will purge Jerusalem (and make it) holy as it was even from the beginning, (for) nations to come from the ends of the earth to see his glory, *to bring as gifts her children who had been driven out,* and to see the glory of the Lord with which God had glorified her. And he will be a righteous king over them, taught by God. There will be no unrighteousness among them in his days, for all shall be holy, and their king shall be the Lord Messiah. (*Pss. Sol.* 17:26–32—emphasis added)[205]

Pitre is quite right to suggest that the "ingathering will be complete…not only when Israel comes home, but when the Gentiles bring the exiles home by coming 'from the ends of the

---

[205] Translations of the Psalms of Solomon are taken from Robert B. Wright, *The Psalms of Solomon: A Critical Edition of the Greek Text* (New York: T&T Clark, 2007).

earth' themselves."[206] In other words, when the Gentile nations are converted to YHWH-worship and flock unto Jerusalem, they will "bring as gifts her [Israel's] children who had been driven out" (*Pss. Sol* 17:31). This then illuminates Paul's Gentile mission in Romans. Moreover, echoes of Jer 23 and Isa 11 can faintly be heard, as it is the righteous Davidic king who will have the Gentile nations serving him under his yoke in Jerusalem. I have already shown that both Jeremiah and Isaiah have the restoration of all twelve tribes in mind.

4.3.6. The Assumption of Moses

Originally composed under Antiochus Epiphanes then redacted in the first part of the first century, the *Assumption of Moses* (also called the *Testament of Moses*) recasts the events found in Deut 31–34.[207] Early on in the narrative, he writes:

> Then God will remember them because of the covenant, which he made with their fathers, and he will openly show his compassion. And in those times *he will inspire a king to have pity on them and send them home to their own land.* Then some parts of the tribes will arise and come to their appointed place, and they will strongly build its walls. Now the *two tribes* will remain steadfast in their former faith, sorrowful and sighing because they will not be able to offer sacrifices to the Lord of their fathers. *But the ten tribes will*

---

[206] Pitre, *Jesus, the Tribulation, and the End of the Exile*, 83.
[207] Nickelsburg, *Jewish Literature Between the Bible and the Mishnah*, 74. Chapters 6 and 7 are understood to be a first century CE interpolation.

> *grow and spread out among the nations during the time of their captivity. (T. Mos.* 4:5–9—emphasis added)[208]

The Deuteronomic curses seem to provide a proper framework for understanding this passage (cf. 4:3). After the destruction of Jerusalem and its temple by the "King from the east" (i.e., Babylon, 3:1), the exiled southern tribes will repent, God will remember the covenant, and will inspire a king to send them home. Here we see the well known motif of sin (breaking the covenant), exile (punishment and separation from true YHWH-worship), and return to the land (deliverance).

Most significant for the purposes of our study is the fact that the author juxtaposes the southern tribes of Jews with the northern tribes who will evidently "grow and spread out among the nations during the time of their captivity" (*T. Mos.* 4:9). This suggests an understanding that the Assyrian exile was considered to be ongoing in the late Second-Temple period and separate from the Babylonian exile.

4.4. Dead Sea Scrolls

The early expectation of the end of the exile is also found in the literature of Qumran. These writings combined restorative-eschatological concerns with an exegesis of Israel's Scripture. Thus, this demonstrates that many during the Second-Temple period were still interested in the teaching of the Torah, while also holding to ardent eschatological expectations, which included the hope for Israel's restoration and return from exile.

---

[208] All translations of the *Assumption of Moses* are those of J. Priest, *Old Testament Pseudepigrapha*, ed. J. H. Charlesworth; 2 vols (New York: Doubleday, 1983), 1.929.

4.4.1. 1QM (*Milẏamah or War Scroll*)

In 1QM, Israel's return from exile is depicted as a gathering for a final eschatological war:

> The sons of Levi, sons of Judah, and the sons of Benjamin, the exiled of the wilderness, shall wage war against them [...] against all their bands, when the exiled sons of light return from the desert of the nations to camp in the desert of Jerusalem. (1QM 1:1–3)[209]

Here I agree with Davies, and more recently Pitre, who have both argued that this passage suggests a reunification of the northern tribes with representatives from the Babylonian exiles.[210] That is, the juxtaposition of the three tribes (i.e., Judah, Benjamin, and part of Levi, who are those who returned from the Babylonian Exile) with those who "return[ed] from the desert of the nations" seems to suggest this to be the case. This is especially so, given that the phrase "sons of light" is used elsewhere in this particular text to refer to all twelve tribes of Israel.

Moreover, it should be pointed out that the writer seems to join the return-from-exile motif with the wilderness motif. As others have pointed out,[211] the writer seems to be echoing Isa 40:3 by using "the voice...in the wilderness" as a sign for Israel's ingathering. I have already demonstrated that Isaiah had both houses of Israel in mind. Finally, I should also note that we have

---

[209] All translations of 1QM are those of Philip R. Davies, *1QM: The War Scroll from Qumran* (Rome: Biblical Institute, 1969).

[210] Davies, *War Scroll from Qumran*, 114; Pitre, *Jesus, the Tribulation, and the End of the Exile*, 115.

[211] Joel Marcus, *The Way of the Lord: Christological Exegesis of the Old Testament in the Gospel of Mark* (Louisville: Westminster/John Knox, 1992), 23.

seen this "wilderness" motif before in Sir 48:10, where we saw Elijah depicted as the restorer of the twelve tribes of Israel.

4.4.2. 4Q174 (4QFlor, MidrEschata)

The document, 4Q174 (4QFlor, MidrEschata), is a *pesharim Midrash* on eschatology. The fragmentary text dates roughly to the end of the first century BCE.[212] It gives us insight into the realm of Second-Temple Judaism's eschatological views, thus providing a fitting framework of restoration by a last day Davidic King.[213] Depicting the community as righteous exiles in the wilderness, it seems to quote a portion of Ezek 37:23: "They shall never again defile themselves with their idols." Remarkably, the end of that very verse in the biblical narrative speaks of the restoration of Israel: "I will save them from all the apostasies into which they have fallen, and will cleanse them. Then they shall be my people, and I will be their God" (v. 23b). Unfortunately, the text of 4Q174 is fragmentary and hard to piece together. However, if the writer shares in the restoration motif of Ezek 37, then it would prove significant for our study, since Ezekiel posited the return of both houses of Israel. Moreover, others have pointed out that in 4Q174, it is possible that the restoration of Israel is implicit, but unstated by the hope for the restored temple (see 4Q174 frag. 1 col. I, 21, 2, lines 1–7).[214]

---

[212] Nickelsburg, *Jewish Literature Between the Bible and the Mishnah*, 75.

[213] Most Scholars support the Davidic King interpretation—see, e.g., Vermes, *Dead Sea Scrolls*, 525–26; John J. Collins, *The Scepter and the Star*, ABRL (New York: Doubleday, 1995), 61; Lawrence H. Schiffman, *Reclaiming the Dead Sea Scrolls*, ABRL (New York: Doubleday, 1995), 325–26.

[214] Pitre, *Jesus, the Tribulation, and the End of the Exile*, 100–01.

4.4.3. *4Q385, 4Q386, and 4Q388*[215]

The Qumran writings known as Pseudo-Ezekiel (i.e., particularly 4Q385, 4Q386, and 4Q388)[216]—which date to the first century BCE[217]—are said to include the earliest example of an "eschatological resurrection of the dead" [218] interpretation of Ezekiel's vision of the valley of dry bones (see Ezek 37:1–14).[219] Though it is possible that there were varying interpretations by the first century BCE, I think any attempt to change this vision of Israel's restoration into something more concrete is quite superfluous.[220] The language in these fragments still very much contains obvious references to the restoration of Israel.

In 4Q385, fragment 1 (which overlaps with 4Q386 and 4Q388), the writer seems to confirm the primacy of Israel's covenant: "[For I am the Lord] who redeems my people, giving them the covenant" (line 1). Afterwards, the prophet asks, "when these things will come to be," and when will the righteous Israelites be "recompensed for their piety," i.e., rewarded for their faithfulness (lines 2–3). The Lord answers that "I will make it manifest to the children of Israel and they will know that I am the Lord" (line 4). Immediately following this claim is an abridged

---

[215] Translations of 4Q385, 4Q386, and 4Q388 are either those of Devorah Dimant, or they are based of the Hebrew texts found in Devorah Dimant, *Parabiblical Texts Part 4: Pseudo-Prophetic Texts* (Oxford: Clarendon Press, 2001), 7–95.

[216] 4Q391 is not relevant to our study.

[217] Vermes, *Dead Sea Scrolls*, 611.

[218] Dimant, *Parabiblical Texts*, 9. She posits that Pseudo-Ezekiel speaks of a future "bodily" resurrection. Moreover, she posits that it is the first known alternative interpretation to the "Restoration of Israel" motif found in the Hebrew Bible version of Ezek 37.

[219] Vermes, *Dead Sea Scrolls*, 611.

[220] Furthermore, whether or not the New Testament writer's actually reworked Ezekiel, as proof of a "bodily" resurrection is debatable. A discussion on the matter is not within the scope of this study.

account of Ezek 37:1–14, in which Ezekiel is told to prophesy: "Let them be joined bone to its bone and joint," and "that skin may cover them," that the "four winds of heaven blow breath upon them," at which time "a large crowd will live and bless the Lord" (lines 5–8). Additionally, in 4Q386, fragment 1, the prophet notes: "the land of Israel is dry" (lines 1–2). This causes the prophet to ask, "when the people will be gathered" (line 3), for which he receives an answer that a "son of Belial will rule over the land and oppress it" until the Lord "leads his own sons out of Memphis" (lines 3–5). It is at that time that the earth will once again be restored as "it was in the days of old" (lines 5–8).

These references seem considerable enough to suggest the importance of the restoration motif found in Ezekiel's vision in the Second-Temple period after the Babylonian exile was over. Moreover, it suggests that the themes of exile and restoration were prevalent in the first century BCE. Finally, it suggests that this portion of Ezekiel was being reworked around the current pressing historical-political situation in the late Second-Temple period, which still had restoration and return from exile fully in view. If the writer of these fragments were indeed adopting the same restoration interpretation as Ezek 37, then it would have also likely included the return of both houses of Israel.

4.5. Philo

Dating between 25 BCE and 50 CE, the Hellenistic Jewish philosopher Philo of Alexandria seems to have envisioned a future day when restorative liberty would come to all and Israel would finally return from exile. In these words of Moses, Philo says:

> For even though they dwell in the uttermost parts of the earth, in slavery to those who led them away captive, one signal, as it were, one day will bring liberty to all. This

> conversion in a body to virtue will strike awe into their masters, who will set them free, ashamed to rule over men better than themselves. When they have gained this unexpected liberty, those who but now were scattered in Greece and the outside world over islands and continents will arise and post from every side with one impulse to the one appointed place, guided in their pilgrimage by a vision divine and superhuman unseen by others but manifest to them as they pass from exile to their home. (*Praem.* 28–29. 164–69)
>
> Everything will suddenly be reversed, God will turn the curses against the enemies of these penitents, the enemies who rejoiced in the misfortunes of the nation and mocked and railed at them...Then those of them who have not come to utter destruction, in tears and groans lamenting their own lapse, will make their way back with course reversed to the prosperity of the ancestral past. (*Praem.* 29. 169–70)[221]

Though Philo seems to have understood restoration symbolically as a return of all people to the Torah—no doubt a product of Hellenistic Jewish Philosophy—these words still show an instance of a first-century expected shift of the present order of things. This no doubt involved the return of all exiled captives.

4.6. Josephus

Regarding Israel's hope for the end of the exile and their future restoration, Josephus is a bit ambiguous. Quite possibly this is because, to write about Israel's expectation of restoration under a reestablished Davidic kingship would certainly be an offense to

---

[221] Translations of Philo are taken from F. H. Colson, *Philo VIII* (Cambridge: Harvard University Press, 1939), 417–21.

Rome (i.e., Josephus likely wrote between 37–100 CE under Roman rule). Nevertheless, I think Josephus can be of some value to our study. He writes: "Wherefore there are but two tribes in Asia and Europe subject to the Romans, while the ten tribes are beyond [the] Euphrates till now, and are an immense multitude, and not to be estimated by numbers" (*Ant.* 11.133).

Of course, Josephus's comment shows that there was a distinction being made in the first century between the southern and northern tribes. Additionally, it shows that though Jews were back in the land, there was an ongoing concern and expectation for the return of the northern tribes. Moreover, his reference to the tribes of Benjamin and Judah as well as the Levites (*Ant.* 11.8; 11.133) and the northern tribes (*Ant.* 11.133) seems to agree with Ezra's description of the inauguration of Israel's restoration describing the return of the tribes of Judah and Benjamin (and some members of the tribe of Levi) to the land.

Finally, Staples' observation concerning Josephus's distinctive terminology provides support to my argument that the northern tribes were in view and that first century Jews were probably making the same distinction. That is, as Staples has pointed out, Josephus used "Ἰσραηλίτης 188 times in the first eleven books of the Antiquities—books dealing with the pre-exilic and exilic periods" and used "Ἰουδαῖος 1,190 times" mostly in his post-exilic work. [222] This is also supported by Josephus's other observation: "The Jews...that is the name they are called by from the day that they came up from Babylon, which is taken from the tribe of Judah" (*Ant.* 11.173).

---

[222] Staples, "A Fresh Look at Romans 11:25–27," 376. See also Josephus, *Ant.* 11.173.

4.7. Conclusion

I have shown that repeated distinctions are made between the northern and southern tribes in both Israel's Scriptures and early Jewish literature. In all cases, it is both houses of Israel, which are expected to be restored. Moreover, this restoration was to be coterminous with the promised end of exile, which also always anticipated the return of both houses of Israel and assumed that as long as parts of Israel's twelve tribes remained scattered, then the promise of return from exile remained unfulfilled.

Moreover, the cumulative weight of evidence seems to suggest that the end of exile was indeed a Second-Temple expectation. Though I do not contend that the nuances of such an expectation were monolithic, it is highly likely that these Second-Temple literary works and this early restoration expectation influenced Paul to one degree or another. That is, Paul most likely grew up in such an environment, and thus, shared in the Second-Temple milieu of the return from exile. Thus, after his conversion, he likely came to rework this expectation—in all its competing forms— around his belief that Jesus was Israel's Messiah. Therefore, if the apostle Paul shared in this early Jewish expectation as Wright also posits,[223] then it is highly likely that Paul—in his appropriation of Hos 1:9–10 and 2:23 in Rom 9:24–26—understood his mission to the Gentiles to also be a means of rescuing the northern tribes from exile. That is, I posit that for the apostle Paul, the Gentile nations coming to salvation is one and the same with the restoration of the northern tribes back into the land. I will now turn my attention to this matter.

---

[223] Wright, *Paul and the Faithfulness of God*, 1049–265.

Chapter 5
PAUL'S APPROPRIATION OF HOS 1:9–10 AND 2:23 IN ROM 9:24–26

In agreement with the methodological procedure that I proposed in chapter 2, this chapter will now investigate Paul's use of Israel's Scriptures in Rom 9. My intent is to examine analogous structural characteristics that will reveal possible allusions and echoes, which will provide support to my overall thesis. Thus, it will be necessary to compare those texts that are relevant to the "overall narrative" with the LXX. Additionally, the examination of possible allusions and echoes will require the employment of Hays's "seven criteria." Moreover, an exegesis of the whole of Rom 9 and select sections of Rom 11 will be necessary. This anomalous, but obligatory departure from the heart of our thesis—i.e., vv. 24–26—will likewise involve the detection of both echoes and allusions. Therefore, before discussing the verses in question, the covering of this much ground will be essential in order to provide us with Paul's appropriate contextual framework and the overall narrative structure of his discourse. To put it candidly, I suggest that Paul's mindset was thoroughly consistent throughout his entire letter to the Romans–i.e., his primary concern was YHWH's faithfulness to the whole nation of Israel. Thus, this agenda will then lead to the climax of my argument.

Finally, my analysis in this chapter will demonstrate that Paul's appropriation of Hos 1:9–10 and 2:23 in Rom 9:25–26 was neither a radical misreading nor an attempt to change the meaning away from the original context—i.e., the northern tribes. Moreover, nor was it a methodical attempt to appropriate the verses toward a detached group called the Gentiles—i.e., they were not detached in Paul's mind. Instead, it was a deliberate hermeneutical scheme designed to show that the ingathering of the Gentile nations also meant the ingathering of the northern tribes, and thus the end of Israel's exile. It was a time of universal restoration for all.

5.1. Rom 9:1–5

> I am speaking the truth in Christ—I am not lying; my conscience confirms it by the Holy Spirit—I have great sorrow and unceasing anguish in my heart. For I could wish that I myself were accursed and cut off from Christ for the sake of my own people, my kindred according to the flesh. They are Israelites, and to them belong the adoption, the glory, the covenants, the giving of the law, the worship, and the promises; to them belong the patriarchs, and from them, according to the flesh, comes the Messiah, who is over all, God blessed forever. Amen.

Paul commences his elucidation by confirming the historical legitimacy and primacy of Israel according to the flesh: "to them belong the adoption, the glory, the covenants, the giving of the law, the worship, and the promises; to them belong the patriarchs, and from them, according to the flesh, comes the Messiah" (Rom 9:4–5). Commentators agree that Rom 9:3 contains a faint intertextual echo of Exod 32:32.[1] As Wagner briefly mentions, it is an "example of Moses interceding for Israel...Paul expresses his passionate love for his kin κατὰ σάρκα...wishing himself cut off from Christ, even as Moses had prayed that God might blot him

---

[1] Wagner, *Heralds*, 45; James D.G. Dunn, *Romans 9–16*, WBC 38B (Dallas: Word, 1988), 525, 539; Schreiner, *Romans*, 480.

out of his book rather than refuse to forgive Israel's worship of the golden calf (Exod 32:32)."[2]

While the English translation reveals no verbal similarity between Rom 9:3 and Exod 32:32, the availability, thematic coherence, historical plausibility, and history of interpretation of this echo are substantial.[3] Consider the following:

Figure 5.1: Exod 32:32 in Rom 9:3

Exodus 32:32 LXX	Rom 9:3
καὶ νῦν εἰ μὲν ἀφεῖς αὐτοῖς τὴν ἁμαρτίαν ἄφες εἰ δὲ μή ἐξάλειψόν με ἐκ τῆς βίβλου σου ἧς ἔγραψας	ηὐχόμην γὰρ ἀνάθεμα εἶναι αὐτὸς ἐγὼ ἀπὸ τοῦ Χριστοῦ ὑπὲρ τῶν ἀδελφῶν μου τῶν συγγενῶν μου κατὰ σάρκα

Figure 5.2: Exod 32:32 in Rom 9:3 (English)[4]

Exodus 32:32 LXX	Rom 9:3
And now if you will forgive their sin and if you will not forgive; erase me from the book that you have written.	For I could pray for myself to be anathema away from Christ on behalf of my brothers my countrymen according to the flesh.

---

[2] Wagner, *Heralds*, 45.

[3] Though notably absent of "volume," this echo meets the following criteria: Availability: Paul undoubtedly had access to the whole book of Exodus; Recurrence: Paul alludes to or echoes Exodus elsewhere, e.g., Exod 33:19 in Rom 9:15 and Exod 9:16 in Rom 9:22–23; Thematic Coherence: Paul's intercession for Israel is analogous to Moses interceding for Israel; Historical Plausibility: Paul's readers were undoubtedly familiar with the story of Moses's intercession; History of Interpretation: Dunn, Schreiner, and Wagner have all posited an echo of Exod 32:32 in Rom 9:3; Satisfaction: satisfies the overall themes of unbelief and rejection in face of miraculous signs.

[4] In this chapter, all Greek to English translations are my own.

Paul here echoes Exodus, not with verbosity, but by employing a common *leitmotif*. It is through the sacrifice of some that Israel is preserved (e.g., Isa 55:5; 4 Macc 17:22). Dunn remarks, just "as Moses was willing to stake all on God's faithfulness to the covenant...so Paul stakes his all on God's continued faithfulness to his covenanted people."[5]

Concerning the plural use of "covenants,"[6] commentators posit that Paul had in mind a specific chronological order of covenants, which are mentioned in Israel's Scripture—e.g., the covenants to Abraham (Gen 15–17), at Mount Sinai (Exod 19:5–6), at Moab (Deut 29–31), at Mount Ebal and at Mount Gerizim (Josh 8:30–35), and to David (2 Sam 23:5).[7] However, others think that by "covenants" Paul means as it was "first given to Abraham and then renewed with Isaac and Jacob—the covenant(s) with the fathers."[8] However, it was also customary for Paul to speak of two covenants, as he does in Gal 4:24. I suggest that this could easily be the case here.

The "old" or "first" covenant was made to Israel. However, though the reach of the new covenant would be extended or transcend beyond the scope of normative ethnic boundaries, it was also promised to the houses of Israel and Judah (Jer 31:31–34). Thus, the language is clear. These covenants (along with the other promises) belong to Israel "according to the flesh" (κατὰ σάρκα, Rom 9:3). It is then important to reinforce my argument from chapter 1. The apostle to the Gentiles is not speaking of a "new Israel" or a "spiritual Israel," but for him, Israel continues to be

---

[5] Dunn, *Romans 9–16*, 532.

[6] Adoption, glory, giving of the law, worship and the promises are also important; but covenant is most significant for our study.

[7] See esp. Cranfield, *Romans*, 462; Moo, *Romans*, 563; Fitzmyer, *Romans*, 546.

[8] Dunn, *New Perspective on Paul*, 435.

Israel. That is, rather than the creation of a "new Israel," Gentile believers are now simply being assimilated into the covenant community of Israel. The displacement of one ethnic identity with another is not what is in view. Certainly, the expansion of the new covenant community is in view, but Paul's point is that it is a people not limited by race (Rom 2:25–3:31). As Hays points out: "Into that one Israel Gentile Christians...have now been absorbed."[9] And Dunn likewise affirms:

> These blessings are Israel's blessings in which Gentile believers have been given part. They have not been transferred from Israel to some other body. Gentiles have not been given a share in them at Israel's expense. By obvious implication the same applies in the case of the "covenants" of 9:4. The covenant(s) in view here are Israel's, and continue to be Israel's. The Gentile believers have been given a share in Israel's covenant blessings. *There is no thought that Gentile believers have superseded Israel, that Israel has forfeited these covenants, or that a new covenant excludes Israel.* For Gentile believers to have received a share in the covenants means that they have been given to share in Israel. (emphasis added)[10]

Though Gentiles in Paul's time were entering into Israel's blessings—evident by Paul's terminological appropriation of Israel's election towards his Gentile churches[11]—the covenants are

---

[9] Hays, *Echoes*, 96–97.

[10] Dunn, *New Perspective on Paul*, 435.

[11] Wagner, *Heralds*, 45n8. See for an example of this, "υἱοί (8:14, 19); υἱοθεσία (8:15, 23; cf. 9:4); τέκνα θεοῦ (8:16, 21); ἀγαπῶσι (8:28, 37; cf. ἀγαπητοῖς θεοῦ, 1:7); πρόθεσις (8:28); προγινώσκω (8:29); προορίζω (8:29); καλέω (8:30); κλητός (8:28, 30); ἐκλεκτῶν θεοῦ (8:33); ἀγάπη (8:35, 39)."

still indeed Israel's. Dunn suggests that Paul's words in 9:4 are "deliberately chosen to remind the predominantly Gentile audience that the blessings they share are Israel's blessings."[12] Thus, despite the contemporaneous problem of Israel's unbelief, Paul still affirms the continuance of Israel's blessings—most notably including the covenant(s) from which the Gentiles now also benefit.

It is also noteworthy that Paul here—by speaking primarily of the grander national entity of "Israel" rather than only "Jews"—has changed his terminology from what we see elsewhere in Romans (e.g., Rom 1:16; 2:9–10, 28–29). That is, Paul's use of the designation Ἰσραηλῖται (Rom 9:4) suggests that he saw a distinction between the expressions "Israelite" and "Jew."[13] Thus, what is in play here is an emphasis on the "whole corporate-covenant community of Israel" (i.e., all twelve tribes), and not only on the descendants of those who had returned from Babylonian exile (i.e., Jews). Of this Dunn says: "The choice of title is obviously deliberate, 'Israelite' being preferred to 'Jew.' 'Israel' was clearly established in scriptural thought as the name equally of the covenant people and of the covenanted land…Paul uses it…as the people of the covenant first made with Abraham and renewed with Jacob."[14]

Thus, for Paul, God had not abandoned the promises made through the prophets to the patriarchs of Israel (Rom 1:2; 9:6; 11:1, 11–12, 29; 15:8). The Ἰσραηλῖται were the carriers of those promises. As Dunn observes, "From them, according to the flesh,

---

[12] Dunn, *Romans 9–16*, 522. Particularly he points out Paul's use of υἱοθεσία (8:15; 23), δόξα (8:18,21), and ἐπαγγελία (4:13–14, 16)."

[13] A noteworthy observation is that the terms "Ἰσραήλ" and "Ἰσραηλῖται" are not used until Rom 9:4, then recurrently in the remainder of 9–11 (e.g., Rom 9:6, 27, 31; 10:19, 21; 11:1, 2, 7, 25, 26). However, forms of "Ἰουδαῖος" or "Ἰουδαῖοι" are only used again in Rom 9:24 and 10:12.

[14] Dunn, *Romans 9–16*, 533.

came the Messiah, who had descended from David according to the flesh." (Rom 9:5; cf. 1:3) And thus, Ἰσραηλίτης is likely "chosen by Paul to evoke his people's sense of being God's elect, the covenant people of the one God."[15]

So then, with this in mind, what is the central contextual thesis of Paul's theology in Rom 9? Simply put, it has to do with the problem of Israel's blindness, which in turn will demand an answer to an interrelated question: what then is the nature of Abraham's seed (9:8)? The fact is that much of Israel has failed to recognize their Messiah. However, at this point Paul has not yet fully articulated his distress. By terminologically appropriating Israel's election for Gentile churches, Paul has caused the issue of God's faithfulness to Israel to reach a boiling point. One must ask: why is Paul comfortable with such a reading of Israel's election? Moreover, how is it that Paul can still affirm the continuance of Israel's blessings while also appropriating them for Gentile churches? My suggestions shall be made clear by the end of this chapter, as other ground must be covered before a precise answer can be formulated.

5.2. Rom 9:6–18

> It is not as though the word of God had failed. For not all Israelites truly belong to Israel, and not all of Abraham's children are his true descendants; but "it is through Isaac that descendants shall be named for you." This means that it is not the children of the flesh who are the children of God, but the children of the promise are counted as descendants. For this is what the promise said, "about this time I will return and Sarah shall have a son." Nor is that all; something similar happened to Rebecca when she had

---

[15] *Ibid.*, 526.

> conceived children by one husband, our ancestor Isaac. Even before they had been born or had done anything good or bad (so that God's purpose of election might continue, not by works but by his call) she was told, "The elder shall serve the younger." As it is written, "I have loved Jacob, but I have hated Esau." What then are we to say? Is there injustice on God's part? By no means! For he says to Moses, "I will have mercy on whom I have mercy, and I will have compassion on whom I have compassion." So it depends not on human will or exertion, but on God who shows mercy. For the scripture says to Pharaoh, "I have raised you up for the very purpose of showing my power in you, so that my name may be proclaimed in all the earth." So then he has mercy on whomever he chooses, and he hardens the heart of whomever he chooses.

"It is not as though the word of God had failed" (Rom 9:6a). No doubt Paul expounded a gospel to the Gentiles that was also the fulfillment of Israel's covenant promise. That promise had continued forward in a direct succession from Abraham, to Isaac, to Jacob, and on through Moses up until Paul's own time, whereby it was now reaching its ultimate significance in the work of the Messiah under Paul's Gentile mission (Rom 9:6–18). It is precisely at this point that we discover the existence of a narrative substructure to Paul's argument in Rom 9; thus here Hays's suggestion that a discourse "has meaning only as an unfolding of the meaning of the story."[16] Here, Paul relies upon his acquaintance with Israel's narrative to frame his own theology about how Israel and the Gentiles have been brought together in the covenant purposes of God. That is, beginning in Rom 9:4, Paul commences his discourse by retelling the covenant story of Israel.

---

[16] Hays, *Faith of Jesus Christ*, 22.

After confirming their historical legitimacy, Paul begins with the call of Abraham (Rom 9:7–12), proceeds to Isaac and to Jacob (Rom 9:7–12), moves on to Moses (esp. the quotation of Exod 33:19 in Rom 9:15), followed by the contextual application of God's sovereign choice as it concerns Israel's historical cry for release from exile and the restoration of Jerusalem after the consequences of conquest and captivity (i.e., the potter and clay metaphor of Jer 18:1–8; Isa 29:16; 45:9; 64:8, which are used as a scriptural setting for Rom 9:19–23). Finally, the themes of Israel's restoration and return-from-exile are further evoked by the use of Hos 1:9–10; 2:23; and Isa 1:9 in Rom 9:25–29. As we shall see, Paul's recollection of Israel's narrative is most significant to our study as God has somehow—through the Messiah—brought about the summation of Israel's story and an end to her exile. Nevertheless, the point I would like to stress as we progress toward the apogee of this study is that Paul does not use Israel's Scriptures as isolated proof-texts. Instead, he knows exactly where he is in Israel's story. It is that *story*, which gives shape to his overall argument in Rom 9. Thus, I posit that Paul has here evoked Israel's narrative—i.e., her covenants and the promise of her restoration—as a robust metanarrative in his efforts toward Israelite and Gentile reconciliation.

It is with this understanding that Paul's discourse begins to fall into place. If God's word has indeed not failed, and if God has not abandoned the promise to Israel, and if the covenants assuredly still belong to Israel, then why would Paul say, "It is not the children of the flesh who are the children of God, but the children of the promise [who] are counted as descendants"? It appears that Paul's thinking is somewhat double-sided. On one side, as already pointed out, the displacement of one ethnic identity with another is not what is in view. However, on the other side, Paul is certainly saying that ethnic heritage has now become, and has always been, a deficient criterion for membership within the covenant community (Rom 2:28–29; 9:6–23). That is, Abraham's promised σπέρμα never was constituted κατὰ σάρκα. It was not "entirely" dependent upon biological genetics (e.g., God rejected Hagar, Ishmael, and Esau, who were all blood associations), but by means of a sovereignly promised progeny, which would ultimately be constituted by God's sovereign choice through Abraham/Sarah, Isaac/Rebecca, and Jacob.

This is significant, because—though the full extent of Paul's argument has not yet been completely developed at this point in chapter 9—the Apostle likely understands that the effects of Israel's exile for violating the covenant has rendered a greater portion of Israel (i.e., the northern tribes) as an impure offspring, unable to lay claim to biological genetics and blood associations anyway. This is evident by Paul's nostalgia for Israel's narrative (i.e., as we shall see, he employs Gen 18; Exod 33:19; Jer 18:1–8; Isa 29:16; 45:9; Mal 1:2–3; Hos 1:9–10; and Hos 2:23 as the context for Rom 9).

Thus, I suggest that in a double-edged sense, Israel's condition has necessitated a call to the Gentiles. That is, both by Israel's blindness (i.e., a partial hardening, Rom 9:18; 11:25) and by the fact that the Assyrian conquest has rendered a greater portion of Israel as non-Israelite. Though Paul argues that a remnant according to the election of grace has been preserved (i.e., Rom 9:29; 11:5), this does not negate the fact that the promise of Israel's restoration involved both houses of Israel, of which one had become "not my people"—hence, the reason the Apostle is so intent on Jewish and Gentile reconciliation.

Paul proceeds by seizing upon the core narrative of Gen 18 with an allusion. In Rom 9:9, he has clearly conflated LXX Gen 18:10 and 18:14:

Figure 5.3: Gen 18:10 and 18:14 in Rom 9:9

Gen 18:10 LXX	Gen 18:14 LXX	Rom 9:9
εἶπεν δέ ἐπαναστρέφων ἥξω πρὸς σὲ **κατὰ τὸν καιρὸν τοῦτον εἰς ὥρας καὶ** ἕξει **υἱὸν Σαρρα** ἡ γυνή σου	εἰς τὸν καιρὸν τοῦτον ἀναστρέψω πρὸς σὲ εἰς ὥρας **καὶ ἔσται τῇ Σαρρα υἱός**	ἐπαγγελίας γὰρ ὁ λόγος οὗτος· **Κατὰ τὸν καιρὸν τοῦτον** ἐλεύσομαι **καὶ ἔσται τῇ Σάρρᾳ υἱός.**

Figure 5.4: Gen 18:10 and 18:14 in Rom 9:9 (English)

Gen 18:10 LXX	Gen 18:14 LXX	Rom 9:9
And he said, coming, I will come to you, **according to this definite space of time**, and **Sarah**, your wife, will have **a son**.	In **this definite space of time,** I will return to you **and Sarah will have a son.**	For the word of promise [is] this; **in this definite space of time**, I will return to you **and Sarah will have a son.**

This group of texts shares an obvious intertextual allusion. It is not a complete quotation, nor is it as faint as an echo. The above comparison shows a remarkable verbal resemblance. Additionally, the "availability," "volume," and "thematic coherence" of this allusion are robust. In terms of "historical plausibility," Paul likely assumes his audience's acquaintance with the outcome of this narrative. That is, the story of Abraham and Sarah was intricately linked to Israel's own election.[17] At the very least, Paul assumes

---

[17] This echo meets the following criteria: Availability: Paul undoubtedly had access to the whole book of Genesis. Recurrence: Paul alludes to or echoes Genesis elsewhere, e.g., Gen 21:12 in Rom 1:12; 7:18; Volume: synonymous phrases such as Κατὰ τὸν καιρὸν τοῦτον and καὶ ἔσται τῇ Σάρρᾳ υἱός; Thematic Coherence: Paul undoubtedly emphasizes that the children of promise would come by his sovereign choice from Abraham/Sarah, which fits with the overall theme; Historical Plausibility: Paul's readers were undoubtedly familiar

his audience had the ability to tease out the details. The children of promise would begin with the faithfulness of Abraham (cf. Rom 4:1–25).

Subsequently, the promise was made to Sarah, and then to Isaac and Rebecca, and finally, to Jacob. Moreover, God is not unjust in his decision. The children of promise would come into existence by his sovereign choice. The point in Rom 9:11–23 is not that God arbitrarily decides to give salvation to some and send others to damnation. Here, the matter of punishment and reward is not even in view. Instead, by his use of Israel's Scriptures, Paul continually advances a corporate-community election over an individual election.[18] Thus, Paul's election in fact has little in common with Calvin and post-Calvin (i.e., Reformed Theology) forms of predestination and election. Instead, God has sovereignly chosen or predestined a specific line from which the children of promise would come (Rom 8:29–30), and that line would ultimately give fuller shape to the covenant community under the Messiah. Thus, the human effort at fulfilling the promise of σπέρμα (seed) through Abraham's slave-girl Hagar was rejected. Likewise, though Abraham had other sons, Isaac was God's

---

with the story of Abraham and Sarah, along with its implications for Israel's election; History of Interpretation: Wagner has posited an echo of Gen 18:10 and 18:14 in Rom 9:9 (see Wagner, *Heralds*, 351); Satisfaction: satisfies the overall theme of Israel's election of grace.

[18] Many scholars reject a Reformed-Calvinist interpretation of Rom 9. It is my contention, and theirs, that if we assume that Paul is speaking of the acceptance or damnation of the individual, then we are misreading of the text. See Wright, *Climax of the Covenant*, 238–39; *Paul and the Faithfulness of God*, 1074; Fitzmyer, *Romans*, 563; Luke T. Johnson, *Reading Romans* (New York: Crossroad, 1997), 140; Ben Witherington, *Paul's Letter to the Romans: A Socio-Rhetorical Commentary* (Grand Rapids: Eerdmans, 2004), 246–59; and Moo, *Epistle to the Romans*, 571.

sovereign choice over Ishmael. Lastly, it was by God's sovereign elective purposes that Jacob was chosen over Esau.

Finally, Paul's quotations of Mal 1:2–3 and Exod 33:19 do not require the application of Hays's criteria. These are both clearly quotations in that they follow the LXX almost exactly.[19] Nevertheless, "thematic coherence" and "historical plausibility" are strong. I submit that these quotations are not employed for mere terminological reasons (i.e., whimsical proof-texting). Instead, the broader context of these quotations suggests that Paul's argument is once again recalling of Israel's entire narrative, hence Hays's metalepsis. For example, in Malachi, we see that Judah has profaned the covenant (Mal 2:10). Thus, the Lord says, he will "cut off from the tents of Jacob" anyone who is faithless (Mal 2:12), because God desires a "godly offspring" (Mal 2:15). As Wagner points out:

> Malachi…indicts the people for their continuing rebellion against God. Only a portion of Israel, "those who fear the Lord" (3:16–21), will experience God's promised redemption. In arguing that in the present time "not all from Israel are Israel," then, Paul is simply extending the logic of a narrative pattern established in the stories of Israel's national origins, a pattern which continued to shape the prophetic understanding of the nature of God's election of Israel.[20]

---

[19] Exod 33:19: ἐλεήσω ὃν ἂν ἐλεῶ καὶ οἰκτιρήσω ὃν ἂν οἰκτίρω; Rom 9:15: Ἐλεήσω ὃν ἂν ἐλεῶ, καὶ οἰκτειρήσω ὃν ἂν οἰκτείρω. Mal 1:2–3: ἠγάπησα τὸν Ιακωβ τὸν δὲ Ησαυ ἐμίσησα; Rom 9:13: Τὸν Ἰακὼβ ἠγάπησα, τὸν δὲ Ἠσαῦ ἐμίσησα.

[20] Wagner, *Heralds*, 51.

Excursus 1: Goyim and Fullness of the Gentiles (Gen 48:19; Rom 11:25–26)

Before continuing on in my exegesis of Rom 9, it is crucial that I digress into a brief excursus on Rom 11, as it is there that Paul gives supplementary shape to his argument in chapter 9. If the children of promise would "ultimately" come through Jacob (i.e., after Abraham/Sarah and Isaac/Rebecca), then what can be said of Jacob?

Jacob was the first Ἰσραηλίτης—a name given to him by God (Gen 32:28). From him, all the twelve tribes of Israel would spring forth. However, at his death, he affirmed that Joseph's sons—Ephraim (the younger) and Manasseh (the eldest)—would carry forward the name of Ἰσραήλ: "In them let my name be perpetuated, and the name of my ancestors Abraham and Isaac; and let them grow into a multitude on the earth" (Gen 48:16b). As for Ephraim's σπέρμα (i.e., a designation for the northern tribes) they would become the "fullness of the Gentiles." Unfortunately, most English translations have rendered Gen 48:19 as "multitude of nations." However, it is worth noting the fact that unlike in v. 16, v. 19 does not use the noun לרב, meaning "multitude." Instead, the noun מלא is used, which means, "fullness." Quite literally, the MT (significant for our study) reads: "His [Ephraim's] seed will become the fullness of the Gentiles" [MT: מלא־הגוים יהיה וזרעו]. In order to illustrate this point further, we must additionally explore Rom 11.

Paul's usage of ὁ πλήρωμα τῶν ἐθνῶν in Rom 11:25b should alert us to the fact that his mission to the Gentiles not only originated in Israel's Scriptures, but was perceived as the fulfillment of Jacob's promise to Joseph about his sons and Israel's future (particularly, the northern tribes). In other words, it was Ephraim that would carry the blessing.

Figure 5:5 Gen 48:19 in Rom 11:25b

Gen 48:19 LXX	Rom 11:25b
τὸ σπέρμα αὐτοῦ ἔσται εἰς πλῆθος ἐθνῶν	ὁ πλήρωμα τῶν ἐθνῶν

Figure 5:6 Gen 48:19 in Rom 11:25b (English)

Gen 48:19 LXX	Rom 11:25b
His seed will become unto a great number of the Gentiles	The fullness of the Gentiles

Here a faint echo can be detected.[21] However, arguably it could be recognized as an allusion. Either way, Paul's wording differs from the LXX by his use of πλήρωμα rather than πλῆθος. Staples suggests that Paul "either had a different Greek version or made the change intentionally, since πλήρωμα...often carries a special apocalyptic or eschatological connotation both in Paul and elsewhere, fitting nicely into the apocalyptic context."[22]

Regardless, the above comparison shows a notable verbal resemblance. Moreover, the "availability," "volume," "historical plausibility," and "thematic coherence" of this allusion are strong.[23] Thus, Paul is most likely echoing Gen 48:19 because he

---

[21] Until Staples's JBL paper, this echo had largely been ignored. The possibility of this echo is not raised in: Cranfield, *Romans*; Dunn, *Romans 9–16*; Hays, *Echoes*; Fitzmyer, *Romans*; Jewett, *Romans*; Schreiner, *Romans*; Moo, *Epistle to the Romans*; Wagner, *Heralds*.

[22] Staples, "A Fresh Look at Romans 11:25–27," 386.

[23] This echo meets the following criteria: Availability: Paul undoubtedly had access to the whole book of Genesis; Recurrence: Paul alludes to or echoes Genesis elsewhere, e.g., Gen 21:12 in Rom 1:12; 7:18 and Gen 18:10, 14 in Rom 9:9; Volume: synonymous phrases such as: πλῆθος ἐθνῶν and ὁ πλήρωμα τῶν ἐθνῶν; Thematic Coherence: Paul is echoing Gen 48:19, because he understands that Ephraim's σπέρμα had become intermingled among the Gentiles as a result of the Assyrian captivity, which fits with the theme of his Gentile mission. Historical Plausibility: Based on what I demonstrated in chapter

understands that Ephraim's σπέρμα had become intermingled among the Gentiles as a result of the Assyrian captivity. Thus, for Paul, the ingathering of the northern tribes is equivalent to the ingathering of the Gentiles. Conversely, the ingathering of the Gentiles is equivalent to the ingathering of the northern tribes. Staples agrees:

> The Gentiles now receiving the Spirit are the fulfillment of Jacob's prophecy—they are Ephraim's seed, they are Israel, restored through the new covenant. God had planned all along that Ephraim's seed would become "the fullness of the nations," so that when Ephraim was restored, it would result also in the redemption of the Gentiles in Abraham's seed.[24]

So then, Paul has framed this echo so that it is even more applicable to his own present circumstances. By employing an all-inclusive hermeneutic, he posits that the ingathering of the Gentile nations is not unconnected from the ingathering of the northern tribes. Paul's mission to the Gentiles was the vehicle whereby Ephraim (i.e., the northern tribes of Israel) would return from among the Gentile nations (Jer 31:1–22), thereby being gathered from exile, restored, and redeemed—and shall I say, by extension, the whole world (i.e., in an atemporal sense). With this in mind, Paul's statement that the children of God are not constituted κατὰ σάρκα—i.e., not dependent on biological birth and blood

---

4 and the fact that Israel's own Scriptures posit Gentile inclusion, Paul's readers were undoubtedly familiar with the narrative; History of Interpretation: Staples has posited an echo of Gen 48:19 in Rom 11:25; Satisfaction: satisfies the overall theme of Israel's election and Gentile inclusion as we have shown elsewhere (e.g., Isa 11).

[24] Staples, "A Fresh Look at Romans 11:25–27," 387.

relations—takes on a new significance. Furthermore, it explains why Paul has evoked Israel's restoration narrative in his efforts toward Jewish and Gentile reconciliation.

Thus, God's word has indeed not failed, nor has God rejected his people whom he foreknew (Rom 9:6; 11:1–2). In fact, God's faithfulness to Israel has been confirmed. God has now saved "all Israel" (Rom 9:26) by reconciling Ephraim (i.e., the northern tribes). Moreover, God in his sovereignty had performed double duty as the restoration of Ephraim also meant the ingathering of the "fullness of the Gentiles."

Excursus 2: Paul's Olive Tree Metaphor (Rom 11:17–24)

> If the part of the dough offered as first fruits is holy, then the whole batch is holy; and if the root is holy, then the branches also are holy. But if some of the branches were broken off, and you, a wild olive shoot, were grafted in their place to share the rich root of the olive tree, do not boast over the branches. If you do boast, remember that it is not you that support the root, but the root that supports you. You will say, "Branches were broken off so that I might be grafted in." That is true. They were broken off because of their unbelief, but you stand only through faith. So do not become proud, but stand in awe. For if God did not spare the natural branches, perhaps he will not spare you. Note then the kindness and the severity of God: severity toward those who have fallen, but God's kindness toward you, provided you continue in his kindness; otherwise you also will be cut off. And even those of Israel, if they do not persist in unbelief, will be grafted in, for God has the power to graft them in again. For if you have been cut from what is by nature a wild olive tree and grafted, contrary to

nature, into a cultivated olive tree, how much more will these natural branches be grafted back into their own olive tree. (Rom 11:17–24)

By way of "historical plausibility," and "thematic coherence,"[25] Paul's use of the metaphorical olive tree is an obvious allusion to Jer 11, Isa 17, and Hos 14, of which all depicted the whole house of Israel as an olive tree:

> The Lord once called you, "A green olive tree, fair with goodly fruit;" but with the roar of a great tempest he will set fire to it, and its branches will be consumed. The Lord of hosts, who planted you, has pronounced evil against you, because of the evil that the *house of Israel* and the *house of Judah* have done, provoking me to anger by making offerings to Baal. (Jer 11:16–17—emphasis added)

Moreover, Isaiah said that Tiglath-Pileser III's annihilation of Aram-Damascus (733–732 BCE) and his capture of the northern territories of Israel—which effectively marked the defeat of the northern tribes of Israel—would be like the beating of an olive tree, in which only few would be left in number:

> The fortress will disappear from Ephraim, and the kingdom from Damascus; and the remnant of Aram will be like the glory of the children of Israel, says the Lord of hosts. On that day the glory of Jacob will be brought low, and the fat of his flesh will grow lean. And it shall be as when reapers

---

[25] In terms of Thematic Coherence and Historical Plausibility: Paul likely understood that Israel was the Olive Tree. Israel's own Scriptures were likely in the recesses of his mind, along with the context of these passages. Paul's readers were also undoubtedly familiar with the narrative.

gather standing grain and their arms harvest the ears, and as when one gleans the ears of grain in the Valley of Rephaim. *Gleanings will be left in it, as when an olive tree is beaten— two or three berries in the top of the highest bough, four or five on the branches of a fruit tree, says the Lord God of Israel.* (Isa 17:3–6—emphasis added)

According to Isaiah, the branch of the house of Israel (i.e., Ephraim) was broken off. However, according to Hosea, though once broken off, Ephraim's descendants would eventually be restored from their state of unfaithfulness and their "shoots" would once again "spread out like the olive tree":

I will heal their disloyalty; I will love them freely, for my anger has turned from them. I will be like the dew to Israel; he shall blossom like the lily, he shall strike root like the forests of Lebanon. *His shoots shall spread out; his beauty shall be like the olive tree*, and his fragrance like that of Lebanon. They shall again live beneath my shadow, they shall flourish as a garden; they shall blossom like the vine, their fragrance shall be like the wine of Lebanon. (Hos 14:4–7—emphasis added)

Discovering the identity of the root, shoots, and branches is necessary for properly understanding Paul's olive tree. I suggest that it is highly likely Paul also had in mind Isa 11 when arguing his case in Rom 11:17–24. Isaiah says: "A shoot shall come out from the stump of Jesse, and a branch shall grow out of his roots.... On that day the root of Jesse shall stand as a signal to the peoples; the nations shall inquire of him, and his dwelling shall be glorious" (Isa 11:1, 10).

For Paul, Isa 11:1 and 10 are a picture of the Gentiles putting their hope in a Davidic King. Thus, there should be no doubt that for Paul the "shoot" and "root of Jesse" was Jesus (i.e., the Messiah, the embodiment of YHWH). His quotation of Isa 11:10 in Rom 15:12 should confirm that this is the case.

Figure 5:7 Isa 11:10 in Rom 15:12

Isa 11:10 LXX	Rom 15:12
καὶ ἔσται ἐν τῇ ἡμέρᾳ ἐκείνῃ ἡ ῥίζα τοῦ Ἰεσσαί, καὶ ὁ ἀνιστάμενος ἄρχειν ἐθνῶν ἐπ' αὐτῷ ἔθνη ἐλπιοῦσιν	καὶ πάλιν Ἡσαΐας λέγει· Ἔσται ἡ ῥίζα τοῦ Ἰεσσαί, καὶ ὁ ἀνιστάμενος ἄρχειν ἐθνῶν· ἐπ' αὐτῷ ἔθνη ἐλπιοῦσιν.

Figure 5:8 Isa 11:10 in Rom 15:12 (English)

Isa 11:10 LXX	Rom 15:12
And [there] will be in that day, a root of Jesse and the one arising to rule the Gentiles in him the Gentiles will hope.	And again Isaiah says, [there] will be a root of Jesse and the one arising to rule the Gentiles, in him the Gentiles will hope.

Obviously, the above comparison shows a remarkable verbal resemblance, as it is a near complete quotation. Thus, it is not really necessary to apply any of Hays's criteria. However, the "thematic coherence" and "historical plausibility" of this quotation must be emphasized. Here, Paul relies on his acquaintance with or own mindful reflection of Israel's narrative to frame his olive tree theology. Moreover, his readers were undoubtedly familiar with this same narrative. Thus, Paul is not telling an ahistorical story, which lacked in significance. Instead, he is recalling Isaiah's narrative, which states that after the Lord finishes using his axe (i.e., Assyria) to cut down his tree Israel for their sins (Isa 10:5–

19), or after he finishes using Assyria as a rod to beat his olive tree (Isa 24–25), Ephraim and Judah will be reconciled, and jointly they "will plunder the people of the east" (Isa 11:13–14).

Equally, "on that day" the Gentiles shall put their hope in "the root of Jesse" (Isa 11:1, 10). As already demonstrated in chapter 4, for Paul the gathering of the *outcasts of Israel* and the *dispersed of Judah* is coterminous with the Gentiles putting their hope in "the root of Jesse."

With this in mind, I can now provide a more proper exegesis of Paul's olive tree metaphor. The identity of Paul's root is clear. It is Jesus. Moreover, the identities of the natural branches are clear. They are both houses of Israel. That is, initially, the olive tree consisted of two branches: the house of Israel and Judah. However, Paul points out that some branches were broken off so that the Gentiles might be grafted in. Who is this but the northern tribes? These became the wild or unnatural branches—Gentiles. Equally, they are those who were long ago broken off and scattered among the Gentiles. As Staples points out, these broken off branches were "from the long-forgotten and uncultivated house of Israel, having been broken off and mixed among the Gentiles so long ago."[26] Thus, they are Ephraim's descendants, who would eventually be restored from their state of unfaithfulness and their "shoots" would once again "spread out like the olive tree" (Hos 14:4–7). Therefore, Paul's point is not that Gentiles are a "replacement" of Israel, but that those with whom Ephraim had intermingled would also come to put their hope in the Davidic King (Isa 11:1, 10). That

---

[26] *Ibid.*, 385. Once again, I must point out that until Staples's JBL paper, this suggestion appears to not have been made "formally" within the guild. This interpretation is not considered in: Cranfield, *Romans*; Dunn, *Romans 9–16*; Hays, *Echoes*; Fitzmyer, *Romans*; Jewett, *Romans*; Schreiner, *Romans*; Moo, *Epistle to the Romans*; Wagner, *Heralds*.

is, all branches—regardless of ethnicity—would now be equally in the olive tree.

Thus, Paul has purposely relied upon Jeremiah's, Isaiah's, and Hosea's narrative, which are all about Israel's restoration. Moreover, we have seen that these prophets simultaneously anticipated the ingathering of Israel, along with the Gentile nations. Therefore, Paul's concern for God's faithfulness to Israel and his eschatological language of exile are not mutually exclusive. That is, Paul believes that Israel's promises for the ingathering of the scattered exiles are being realized in his time. However, it is also congruent with his mission, which also involves an eschatological and "once mysterious" ingathering of a Gentile people. For Paul, they are one in the same. We can now return our study of Rom 9.

5.3. Vessels of Wrath and Mercy (Rom 9:19–23)

> You will say to me then, "Why then does he still find fault? For who can resist his will?" But who indeed are you, a human being, to argue with God? Will what is molded say to the one who molds it, "Why have you made me like this?" Has the potter no right over the clay, to make out of the same lump one object for special use and another for ordinary use? What if God, desiring to show his wrath and to make known his power, has endured with much patience the objects of wrath that are made for destruction; and what if he has done so in order to make known the riches of his glory for the objects of mercy, which he has prepared beforehand for glory. (Rom 9:19–23)

Paul is remarkably consistent throughout all of Rom 9—God has exercised his sovereign choice in choosing a line through which the children of promise would come. Here, Paul employs Jeremiah's "potter over the clay" story:

> So I went down to the potter's house, and there he was working at his wheel. The vessel he was making of clay was spoiled in the potter's hand, and he reworked it into another vessel, as seemed good to him. Then the word of the Lord came to me: "Can I not do with you, O house of Israel, just as this potter has done?" says the Lord. "Just like the clay in the potter's hand, so are you in my hand, O house of Israel. At one moment I may declare concerning a nation or a kingdom, that I will pluck up and break down and destroy it, but if that nation, concerning which I have spoken, turns from its evil, I will change my mind about the disaster that I intended to bring on it." (Jer 18:2–8)

Although there is remarkably little verbal resemblance, the "thematic coherence" and "historical plausibility" of this allusion are robust,[27] thus this text is certainly an echo in Paul's argument in Rom 9. As noted before, Paul does not employ these echoes, allusions, or quotations for mere terminological or proof-texting reasons. Instead, their broader context suggests that Paul's argument is once again a recalling of Israel's entire narrative, hence Hays's *metalepsis*. Here, according to the Potter's sovereign choice, the pots (idolatrous and unfaithful Israel) have been smashed, melted down, and molded into something different.

---

[27] In Jer 18:4, the Greek word ἀγγεῖον is chosen for "vessel" instead of σκεῦος, which is used elsewhere (e.g., in Hos 8:8; Rom 9:21). Moreover, in terms of Thematic Coherence and Historical Plausibility: Paul likely understood that Israel was the clay in the potter's hands. Israel's own Scriptures were likely in the recesses of his mind, along with the context of these passages. Paul's readers were also undoubtedly familiar with the narrative.

Commentators agree that Paul, in Rom 9:20, has also made use of the LXX Isa 29:16,[28] as seen in the following comparison:

Figure 5:9 Isa 29:16 in Rom 9:20b

Isa 29:16 LXX	Rom 9:20b
μὴ ἐρεῖ τὸ πλάσμα τῷ πλάσαντι οὐ σύ με ἔπλασας	μὴ ἐρεῖ τὸ πλάσμα τῷ πλάσαντι Τί με ἐποίησας οὕτως;

Figure 5:10 Isa 29:16 in Rom 9:20b (English)

Isa 29:16 LXX	Rom 9:20b
Will not the [thing] fashioned say to the one having fashioned it, you did not make me?	**Will not the [thing] fashioned say to the one having fashioned it**, Why have you made me like this?

Once again, we can see that the "volume," "thematic coherence," and "historical plausibility" of this allusion are robust.[29] Paul has recalled Israel's narrative. His employment of the Potter and clay motif is part of the larger narrative in Isa 28–29. Ephraim (i.e., the northern tribes) would be overwhelmed by Assyria (Isa 28:1–4) and Jerusalem (i.e., the southern tribes) would be besieged (Isa

---

[28] Dunn, *Romans 9–16*, 550–61; Wagner, *Heralds*, 59; Schreiner, *Romans*, 516. All three point out that Paul is also most likely alluding to Isa 45:9.

[29] This echo meets the following criteria: Availability: Paul undoubtedly has access to Isaiah; Volume: synonymous phrases such as: "μὴ ἐρεῖ τὸ πλάσμα τῷ πλάσαντι" and "μὴ ἐρεῖ τὸ πλάσμα τῷ πλάσαντι;" in terms of Thematic Coherence and Historical Plausibility: Paul likely understood that Israel was the clay in the potter's hands. Israel's own Scriptures were likely in the recesses of his mind, along with the context of these passages. Paul's readers were also undoubtedly familiar with the narrative; History of Interpretation: Wagner perceived the echo of Isa 29:16 in Rom 9:20, along with Isa 45:9. For a deeper analysis see, Wagner, *Heralds*, 58–71.

29:1-8). However, a remnant would be spared (Isa 28:5), and blindness would happen in part to Israel (Isa 29:9–16). However, the future holds restoration for all Israel (Isa 29:9–16). Once again, we can see that Paul is at work recalling the promise of Israel's restoration as a robust metanarrative in his own efforts toward Jewish and Gentile reconciliation.

Next, in common diatribe fashion, Paul asks, "What if God...endured with much patience the objects of wrath that are made for destruction?" (9:22). How should we then identify these objects/vessels of wrath and mercy? We can reasonably see that a subtle echo is being evoked.[30] Paul seems to be echoing Hos 8:8. A comparison with LXX might illustrate my position more clearly.

Figure 5:11 Hos 8:8 in Rom 9:21

Hos 8:8 (LXX)	Rom 9:21
κατεπόθη Ισραηλ νῦν ἐγένετο ἐν τοῖς ἔθνεσιν ὡς **σκεῦος** ἄχρηστον	ἢ οὐκ ἔχει ἐξουσίαν ὁ κεραμεὺς τοῦ πηλοῦ ἐκ τοῦ αὐτοῦ φυράματος ποιῆσαι ὃ μὲν εἰς τιμὴν **σκεῦος** ὃ δὲ εἰς ἀτιμίαν;

The above comparison shows that, except for the word "σκεῦος" (usually translated "vessel"), there is remarkably little verbal resemblance, and no direct citation between Rom 9:21 and Hos 8:8. Nevertheless, the "availability," "thematic coherence," and "historical plausibility" of this allusion are robust. Perhaps a look at the English will aid in our evaluation.[31]

---

[30] The possibly of this echo is not considered in the following: Cranfield, *Romans*; Dunn, *Romans 9–16*; Hays, *Echoes*; Fitzmyer, *Romans*; Jewett, *Romans*; Schreiner, *Romans*; Moo, *Epistle to the Romans*; Wagner, *Heralds*; Staples, "A Fresh Look at Rom 11:25–27."

[31] This echo meets the following criteria: Availability: Paul undoubtedly had access to Hosea. This is evident by his use in Rom 9:25–26. Moreover, as we

Figure 5:12 Hos 8:8 in Rom 9:21 (English)

Hos 8:8 LXX	Rom 9:21
Israel is swallowed up: now has become among the Gentiles as a useless **vessel** (or, as a worthless/dishonorable vessel).	Or has not the potter authority [over] the clay to make out of the same lump one **vessel** indeed unto honor and one unto dishonor?

In the English translation, the above comparison is easily seen to be analogous in nature. Thus, I argue that Paul here evokes a "subtle echo" over an allusion, even though there is no concrete intertextual reference. Hosea's "vessels of dishonor" or "worthless vessels" are none other than the divorced and exiled northern tribes of Israel in Hos 8:8.[32]

"And if God desiring to show his wrath, and to make known his power, brought forth in much patience vessels of wrath having been fitted for destruction" (εἰ δὲ θέλων ὁ θεὸς ἐνδείξασθαι τὴν ὀργὴν καὶ γνωρίσαι τὸ δυνατὸν αὐτοῦ ἤνεγκεν ἐν πολλῇ μακροθυμίᾳ σκεύη ὀργῆς κατηρτισμένα εἰς ἀπώλειαν [Rom 9:22]). We must note that ἀπώλεια and ἀπόλλυμι share the same

---

have discussed, he also had access to Isaiah, which also discusses the fashioning of vessels. Volume: There is actually very little, only the synonymous words: σκεῦος and σκεῦος; "Thematic Coherence" and "Historical Plausibility:" Paul likely understood that Israel was the one fashioned into a vessel by the potter's hands. Israel's own Scriptures were likely in the recesses of his mind, along with the context of these passages. Paul's readers would have also undoubtedly been familiar with the narrative; History of Interpretation: unfortunately, I have not yet found another scholar who posits the same thing as I have suggested.

[32] Schreiner wrongly interprets Rom 9:21–22 along the lines of Calvin's and post–Calvinist notions of double predestination to mean individualistic salvation (see *Romans*, 517). Piper provides an interpretation similar to Schreiner; see *Future of Justification*, 192. Conversely, Cranfield, Dunn, and Fitzmyer rightly understand it too be speaking of Israel's historical destiny—see, Cranfield, *Romans*, 493; Dunn, *Romans 9–16*, 558; Fitzmyer, *Romans*, 569.

stem, which does not imply "annihilation," but literally "to be cut off." Paul's point is that God is long-suffering in the threat of his wrath upon the disobedient (i.e., unfaithful Israel, particularly, cut off or divorced Israel). Why? All is made clear in v. 23. Tolerance has been exercised, "so that he might make known the riches of his glory on the vessels of mercy, which he has before prepared unto glory." That is, those whom he has chosen to be his people from among the Gentiles nations, which are one and the same as returning Ephraim, also includes a remnant of believing Jews. These constitute Paul's new covenant community.

Thus, we can see that the crucial flow of Paul's discourse has gone unchanged. By his loose commentary of Exodus, Paul posited that Israel in his own day had become like Pharaoh. Their "partial" hardening was for the very purpose of showing God's redeeming power to all. This was accomplished by Israel's fall. Thus, divorced Ephraim had become a worthless vessel of dishonor for sake of the whole world.

5.4. Rom 9:24–26 "Not My People" (Hos 1:10; 2:23)

> Even us whom he has called, not from the Jews only but also from the Gentiles? As indeed he says in Hosea, "Those who were not my people I will call 'my people,' and her who was not beloved I will call 'my beloved.' And in the very place where it was said to them, 'You are not my people,' they will be called 'sons of the living God'." (Rom 9:24–26)

We have now reached the apogee of our study. Paul's argument in Rom 9:24–26 continues without a significant break from Rom 9:1–23—thus, the reason for my thorough exegesis. Here, Paul applies Hosea's pronouncement—originally made to the northern tribes—to the Gentiles. By reading Hosea's promise of the northern tribes' restoration and ingathering from exile as a word for Gentiles, has Paul radically changed the original meaning? Once again, the broader context of this allusion suggests that Paul is recalling the whole of Israel's narrative (*metalepsis*) and not conducting an exercise in proof-texting. Paul's appropriation of Hosea's words can seem a bit anomalous at first glance. However, when we realize that Paul's Gentile appropriation also adumbrates the ingathering of the northern tribes, the passage become clearer.

J. Paul Tanner has said, "Any attempt to argue that the Hosea quotations were used by Paul in Romans to argue for the inclusion of all ethnic Israelites must certainly be rejected."[33] However, here more than anywhere else, Paul's mention of Gentiles in conjunction with Israel's story makes it clear that he has evoked the northern tribes' narrative—particularly their promise of restoration from exile—as a robust metanarrative in his efforts toward Jewish and Gentile reconciliation. By identifying Gentiles as "not my people" or "not loved," Paul recalls the plight and restoration hopes of his own brethren—i.e., the northern tribes. As Staples puts it, Paul's Gentiles are "Ephraim's seed...being restored from among the nations, being redeemed from its cut-off, Gentile state, becoming 'children of the living God' once again."[34] Thus, Paul's call to the Gentiles is coterminous with God restoring

---

[33] See particularly, 96 n2 in J. Paul Tanner, "The New Covenant and Paul's Quotations from Hosea in Romans 9:25–26," *BibSac* 162 (2005): 95–110. My position should not be confused with the Dispensationalist notion that Hosea quotations in Rom 9:25–26 represent a literal application of the Old Testament text to ethnic national Israel. Instead, my argument is that for Paul, the ingathering of the northern tribes and Gentiles are one in the same with God's planned renewal of covenant relationship. Moreover, I posit that Paul introduces the Hosea texts in Rom 9:25–26 as proof that the events being described were being fulfilled in his own time.

[34] Staples, "A Fresh Look at Romans 11:25–27," 382.

his covenant relationship with the northern tribes (2:19) and his annulling of Israel's covenant curses (Deut 30).

Though commentators do not fully concur with Staples's suggestion as I do, they agree with the suggestion that Paul in Rom 9:24–26 combines sections from "Hos 2:23 LXX (2:25 MT) and Hos 1:10 LXX (2:1 MT)."[35]

Figure 5:13 Hos 1:10 and 2:23 in Rom 9:25–26

Hos 1:10 LXX	Hos 2:23 LXX	Rom 9:25–26
καὶ ἔσται ἐν τῷ τόπῳ οὗ ἐρρέθη αὐτοῖς οὐ λαός μου ὑμεῖς ἐκεῖ κληθήσονται υἱοὶ θεοῦ ζῶντος	καὶ σπερῶ αὐτὴν ἐμαυτῷ ἐπὶ τῆς γῆς καὶ ἐλεήσω τὴν οὐκ-ἠλεημένην καὶ ἐρῶ τῷ οὐ-λαῷ-μου λαός μου εἶ σύ καὶ αὐτὸς ἐρεῖ κύριος ὁ θεός μου εἶ σύ	(25) Καλέσω τὸν οὐ λαόν μου λαόν μου καὶ τὴν οὐκ ἠγαπημένην ἠγαπημένην· (26) καὶ ἔσται ἐν τῷ τόπῳ οὗ ἐρρέθη αὐτοῖς· Οὐ λαός μου ὑμεῖς, ἐκεῖ κληθήσονται υἱοὶ θεοῦ ζῶντος.

---

[35] Cranfield, *Romans*, 499–500; Dunn, *Romans 9–16*, 571–73; Moo, *Epistle to the Romans*, 154. Since these are almost complete quotations, it is not necessary to apply any of Hays's criteria. Nevertheless, Paul's use of Hosea meets the following criteria: Availability: Paul undoubtedly had access to the whole book of Hosea; Volume: Paul uses synonymous phrases such as: "καὶ ἔσται ἐν τῷ τόπῳ οὗ ἐρρέθη αὐτοῖς οὐ λαός μου ὑμεῖς ἐκεῖ κληθήσονται υἱοὶ θεοῦ ζῶντος" and "ἐλεήσω τὴν οὐκ-ἠλεημένην καὶ ἐρῶ τῷ οὐ-λαῷ-μου λαός μου εἶ σύ" in Rom 9:25–26; Thematic Coherence: Paul is using Hosea 1:10 and 2:23, because he understands that his Gentile ministry is a picture of Ephraim's σπέρμα being restored from among the nations, which fits with his theme of ingathering Gentiles; History of Interpretation: Cranfield, Dunn, Moo, and Schreiner all suggest that Paul in Rom 9:24–26 combines sections from Hos 1:10 LXX (2:25 MT) and Hos 2:23 LXX (2:1 MT).

Once again, a look at the English translation will aid our understanding:

Figure 5:14 Hos 1:10 and 2:23 in Rom 9:25–26 (English)

Hos 1:10 LXX	Hos 2:23 LXX	Rom 9:25–26
And in the place where it was said of them not my people you there shall be called sons of the living God.	I will sow her unto myself in the earth and **I will call the not mercy (those not shown mercy),** and **I will say to not my people, you are my people** and they shall say, you are Lord **my God.**	**I will call not my people, my people** and not loved, loved and **in the place where it was said of them not my people you there shall be called sons of the living God.**

It is agreed that v. 25 is an amalgamation of the two LXX clauses, ἐλεήσω τὴν οὐκ-ἠλεημένην and ἐρῶ τῷ οὐ-λαῷ-μου λαός μου εἶ σύ.[36] Here, however, Paul has substituted ἐρῶ for Καλέσω. Wagner suggests that this was intentional to link "earlier occurrences of this verb as a term for divine election in Romans 9:7, 12."[37] Nevertheless, Paul's deviation from the LXX, "I will say" (ἐρῶ) to, "I will call" (καλέσω) validates his emphasis on the effectual call also found in verses 24–26. Furthermore, Paul likewise chooses ἠγαπημένην in place of ἠλεημένην, signifying that those whom were once "not shown mercy" (i.e., MT: לארחמה "Lo-Ruhamah," the northern tribes [Hos 1:6]) are those who were "not loved," but are now "loved." This move seems to be consistent with what Paul has argued earlier in the chapter (i.e.,

---

[36] See also Cranfield, *Romans*, 571; Dunn, *Romans 9–16*, 499.
[37] Wagner, *Heralds*, 80. See also Edward W. Glenny, "The People of God in Romans 9:25–26," *BibSac* 152 (1995): 42–59.

Rom 9:13). Finally, v. 26 seems to agree verbatim with the LXX of Hos 1:10.

What does this suggest? By direct quotation, intentional modification, and by use of the designations "not my people" and "not loved," Paul has posited that the promise of the northern tribes' return from exile in Hosea is coterminous with God's call of Gentiles. Of this, Moo writes:

> Those familiar with the Old Testament might wonder at Paul's application of these prophecies from Hosea to Gentiles, for Hosea was predicting the return of the northern tribes of Israel, not the conversion of the Gentiles. This is one example of the many places in which Paul does not seem to quote the Old Testament in accordance with its original meaning.[38]

I agree with Moo about Hosea's prediction, but I am strongly opposed to the assertion that Paul does not hold to the original meaning. What Paul is doing here is a bit complex and double-sided. It is clearly evident that the Apostle wished to break down the barriers that divided Jews and Gentiles. Thus, Paul is seeking to address the question, "how have Israel and the Gentiles been brought together in the covenant purposes of God?" This is also evident elsewhere (i.e., Rom 15:6–7) as Paul is seeking to unite both Jews and Gentiles in Rome around his gospel. In fact, as commentators have pointed out, the "Jew-Gentile dynamic" found in Rom 1:16–17 is in fact "thematic" for the whole book of Romans.[39] Wright has also observed:

---

[38] Moo, *Epistle to the Romans*, 133.

[39] Cranfield, *Romans*, 87–102; Dunn, *Romans 9–16*, 37; Fitzmyer, *Romans*, 98; Jewett, *Romans*, vii; Moo, *Epistle to the Romans*, 63–79; Schreiner, *Romans*, 58–76.

> The presupposition of Paul's argument is that, if there is one God [monotheism]—the foundation of all Jewish belief—there must be one people of God. Were there to be two or more peoples, the whole theological scheme would lapse back into some sort of paganism, with each tribe or race possessing its own national deities.[40]

The identity of Israel and her relationship to Gentiles is something that Paul has quite deliberately allowed to be provoked from what he had begun in Rom 2:25–3:31. Paul is employing an "inclusive" or "all-encompassing" hermeneutic: God's faithfulness is for all. Thus, Paul is including those from the Gentile nations who are now turning to Israel's God through belief in Jesus as the Messiah.

In contrast to Moo, this includes restored Ephraim as well as a faithful remnant of believing Jews (Rom 11:5). Paul's hermeneutic is inclusive of both the circumcised and uncircumcised (Rom 3:27–31), which is now and always has been ultimately a "heart matter" anyway (Rom 2:29; cf. Ezek 44:7). Thus, there is now no basis for judging one group to be inferior over the other. Both Jews and Gentiles are now equal heirs of God's patronage in Christ. "Foreigners" have joined themselves to the YHWH, and his house has now become a "house of prayer for all peoples" (Isa 56:1–8). Significant is the fact that according to Isaiah, when Israel is restored, the outcasts are gathered along with the nations (Isa 56:1–8). To this, I have already demonstrated in chapter 4 that Isaiah's Israel language also applies to the northern tribes. Nevertheless, I posit that verses 25–26 are applied both to the Gentiles and the northern tribes, because Paul's call to the Gentiles is coterminous with God's restoring his covenant relationship with the northern tribes.

---

[40] Wright, *Climax of the Covenant*, 170.

5.5. Hays, Wagner, and Wright on Rom 9:24-26

Finally, our study has sought to adequately address the question: by reading Hosea's promise of the northern tribes' restoration and ingathering from exile as a word to first-century Gentiles, has Paul radically changed the original meaning? In chapter 1, we heard from those who think this is exactly the situation. Likewise, Moo suggests this is the case.[41] Furthermore, Hays has written the following concerning Paul's use of both Hosea in Rom 9:

> Where Hosea clings to the poignant hope of Israel's privileged place despite her "harlotry," Paul deconstructs the oracle and dismantles Israel's privilege; with casual audacity he *rereads the text* as a prophecy of God's intention to embrace Gentiles as his own people. This *hermeneutical coup* is so smoothly executed that Gentile Christian readers might miss its *innovative boldness*—and therefore its *potential scandal* to Jewish readers. Paul is not arguing by analogy that just as God extended mercy to Israel even when Israel was unworthy so also he will extend grace to the Gentiles. Instead, Paul is arguing that God was speaking through the prophet Hosea to declare his intention to call Gentiles to be his own people. It is as though the light of the gospel shining through the text has illuminated a latent sense so brilliant that the opaque original sense has vanished altogether. Or has it? If the quotation is a warrant for the claim made in Rom 9:24 that God has "called us not only from the Jews but also from the Gentiles," then a real ambiguity exists in Paul's use of it…thus, in the first instance [24–26], Paul is reading the prophecy as a promise of Gentile inclusion among God's

---

[41] Moo, *Epistle to the Romans*, 133.

people...[second, in 27–28] Paul now cites a prophecy about Israel.[42] (emphasis added)

What is Hays saying? First, Paul has provided a revisionary reading of Hosea in Rom 9:24–26. In fact, Hays uses strong language and phrasing to describe Paul's appropriation of Hosea, such as: "hermeneutical coup," "innovative boldness," "potential scandal," and "adducing proof texts."[43] Second, Paul's concern, according to Hays, is for Jew and Gentile only. He suggests, "The quotation from Hosea proves that God calls Gentiles, and the quotation from Isaiah proves that he calls Jews."[44] That statement is only partly true. Nonetheless, as Hays correctly points out, "Paul is arguing that God was speaking through the prophet Hosea to declare his intention to call Gentiles to be his own people." Yes, but the question is: why did Paul feel so strongly about using Israel's Scriptures in this way?

Likewise, Wagner calls Paul's appropriation a "surprising reversal"[45] or a "hermeneutic of reversal."[46] He writes:

> It is by means of the appellation "not my people" that Paul gains hermeneutical leverage over the text, wresting from it the astounding conclusion that the promise of return from exile and national restoration for Israel in Hosea is really an announcement of God's embrace of Gentiles as his own people. Paul hyper-extends the logic of reversal inherent in Hosea's salvation oracles, with the result that the scope of "not my people" now embraces not only covenant-breaking

---

[42] Hays, *Echoes*, 67–68.
[43] *Ibid.*
[44] *Ibid.*, 68.
[45] Wagner, *Heralds*, 79–83.
[46] *Ibid.*, 83.

Israel, but also the Gentiles, who once were excluded from God's covenant altogether.[47]

What is Wagner saying? First, Paul is using a "hermeneutic of reversal" and is "misreading...the prophetic oracle."[48] This required "a radical rereading of texts foundational to Israel's understanding of election."[49] Second, Wagner essentially follows Hays in saying: "Hosea's oracles envision not only the redemption of Israel, but also the calling of 'some from among the Gentiles'."[50] I agree, but once again I ask: why did Paul feel so strongly about using Israel's Scriptures in this way?

Finally, Wright has likewise called Paul's appropriation a "shocking inclusion."[51] Wright suggests that Paul's use of Hos 1:9–10 and 2:23 to support Rom 9:25–26 would have been "highly controversial...something that Saul of Tarsus and his kinsfolk according to the flesh would not have expected or approved."[52]

Though I build my case upon the insights of Hays, Wagner, and Wright, I also offer what I think are important correctives. I think Paul had good reasons for doing this. I suggest that in Paul's mind, Hosea's northern tribes had acculturated with nations long ago, thereby losing their identity and effectively becoming "not my people" or the "not loved"—i.e., Gentiles. Thus, Paul believes he is justified in appropriating Hosea in the manner in which he does. Though Hays, Wagner, and Wright might deny it, they seem to have created a superfluous narrowing of Paul's more multifaceted concern for Israel's promises. Paul's Gentile appropriation

---

[47] *Ibid.*
[48] *Ibid.*
[49] *Ibid.*
[50] *Ibid.*, 84.
[51] Wright, *Paul and the Faithfulness of God*, 924.
[52] *Ibid.*, 1185.

adumbrates the ingathering of the northern tribes. Thus, what I am arguing for here should by now be clear: the Gentile nations come to salvation concurrently with the restoration of all Israel and the ingathering of the northern tribes. That is, Paul understands his call to Gentiles to be simultaneously bringing about the ingathering of the northern tribes of Israel, and thus, the redemption of the whole world. He employs a deliberate hermeneutical scheme to show that the ingathering of the Gentile nations also meant the ingathering of the northern tribes, and conversely, the end of Israel's exile. It was a time of universal restoration for all.

Chapter 6
CONCLUSION

In Rom 9:24–26, Paul applies Hosea's pronouncement—originally to the northern tribes—to the Gentiles. The driving motivation of this study has been to answer the question: By reading Hosea's words concerning the northern tribes' promised restoration and ingathering from exile as a word for Gentiles, did Paul radically change the original meaning of Hosea? As I have demonstrated, the answer must be "no!"

I began this study by challenging the normative distinction made between Israel and the church (see chapter 1). I posited that it is not necessarily proper to identify the church as spiritual Israel. Moreover, to interpret Paul's language as a "replacement" or "displacement" model is to constrict the complexity of his argument and it does not fully engage with his intended message. Likewise, perennial arguments of Covenant Theology that have simplified this to "the church as Israel composed of both Jews and Gentiles" are a bit inadequate. Instead, Paul, while affirming God's faithfulness to Israel's covenant promises, understood that their fulfillment must involve *all* twelve tribes of Israel as the prophets had proclaimed. Therefore, Paul was not speaking of a "new Israel" or a "spiritual Israel," but for him, Israel was Israel. That is, rather than the creation of a "new Israel," Gentile believers were being assimilated into a regrouped covenant community of Israel. The displacement of one ethnic identity with another was not what was in view.

Along these lines, I demonstrated that one of the problems in dialogue on this subject is often one of nomenclature. As we saw, many interpreters have assumed that the terms "Israel" or "Israelite" are to be taken as synonyms for the term "Jew." However, the northern tribes of Israel and the southern tribes of Judah were not identical analogues. Instead, Paul's employment of the term Ἰσραηλῖται suggests that he saw a distinction between the designations Israelite and Jew. Thus, what was in play for Paul was the grander national entity of Israel.

With this in mind, Paul's hermeneutical method becomes clearer in explaining just how he was using the Old Testament (particularly, Hos 1:9–10 and 2:23)—originally addressed to the northern tribes of Israel—in the New Testament, and in relation to the Gentiles. As we discovered, Paul was not necessarily interested in creating a historically pristine record of things, but rather a narrative that incorporated both selective and relevant pieces of information from the historical past. Thus, Paul used a conglomeration of both history and theology to shape his narrative. It was this blend of history and theology interacting with each other throughout his narrative. Historically, as I demonstrated in chapter 3, Paul understood that the Assyrians had conquered the northern tribes of Israel. This event likely affected a variety of identity changes whether they remained in Samaria or were deported. Thus, what was likely evident for Paul was that the majority of the northern tribes, became an eclectic mix of people with no discrete national identity. In effect, they became Gentiles. Theologically speaking, Paul relied upon his acquaintance with Israel's narrative to frame his own theology about how Israel and the Gentiles have been brought together in the covenant purposes of God. As I proposed in chapter 2, Paul was not always recalling a particular OT text, but often a portion of the whole narrative itself. Thus, Paul decisively appropriated Israel's narrative in Hosea as the metanarrative toward his mission of Jewish and Gentile reconciliation.

In chapter 4, I sought to support these claims with both Israel's Scriptures and Second-Temple literary sources. By examining Israel's Scriptures, I showed that repeated distinctions were made between the northern and southern tribes. In all cases, it was both houses of Israel that were to be restored to the land. Moreover, this restoration was coterminous with the promised end of exile, which always anticipated the return of both houses of Israel (i.e., all twelve tribes of Israel), and assumed that as long as parts of Israel's twelve tribes remained scattered, then the promise of return from exile remained unfulfilled. Likewise, I demonstrated that this expectation was coterminous with the Davidic King at the time of the New Covenant. Thus, this fact firmly time stamps the event to Paul's first-century ministry.

By examining both Israel's Scriptures and Second-Temple literature, I sought to answer the question: What were the restoration and exile expectations of those living in the Second-Temple period? I also showed that repeated distinctions were made between the northern and southern tribes in early Jewish literature. The cumulative weight of evidence seems to suggest that the end of exile was indeed a Second-Temple expectation. Although I do not contend that the nuances of such an expectation were monolithic, it is highly likely that these Second-Temple literary works along with this expectation influenced Paul to some degree. That is, Paul most likely grew up in such an environment, and thus, shared in the Second-Temple hope of the return from exile. Thus, after his conversion, he likely came to rework this expectation—in all its competing forms—around his belief that Jesus was Israel's Messiah. Therefore, he reflected upon his understanding of this theme in his appropriation of Hos 1:9–10 and 2:23 in Rom 9:25–26. Paul understood his mission to the Gentiles to also be a means of rescuing the northern tribes from exile, thus bringing an end to it. Therefore, for Paul, the Gentile nations coming to salvation was one and the same with the restoration of the northern tribes into the land.

Finally, in chapter 5, I sought to locate this study against the backdrop of well-established intertextual methods. By employing the hermeneutical methods of detection first set forth by Hays, I conducted a brief analysis of the OT context with the intent to reveal analogous structural characteristics. Additionally, I conducted a textual comparison primarily against relevant textual traditions. The outcome provided support to the claim that there is a "narrative substructure" that lies underneath Paul's text in Rom 9, which provides the proper framework for understanding and interpreting his Gentile mission. Thus, Paul's appropriation of Hos 1:9–10 and 2:23 in Rom 9:25–26 was not the result of some whimsical proof-texting on Paul's part, but it was employed to evoke the promise of Israel's restoration as a robust metanarrative in his own efforts toward Jewish and Gentile reconciliation.

BIBLIOGRAPHY

Ambrosiaster. *Ambrosiastri Qui Dicitur Commentarius in Epistulas Paulinas.* CSEL 81.1. Edited by H.J. Vogels. Vienna: Hoelder-Pichler-Tempsky, 1966.

Augustine. *St. Augustine's Writings Against the Manichaeans and Against the Donatists.* Edited by Richard Stothert. Altenmünster: Jazzybee Verlag, 2012.

Baden, Joel. *The Historical David: The Real Life of an Invented Hero.* New York: HarperOne, 2013.

Bakhtin, M.M. *The Dialogic Imagination: Four Essays.* Edited by Michael Holquist. Translated by Caryl Emerson. Austin: University of Texas Press, 1981.

_____. and P.N. Medvedev. *The Formal Method in Literary Scholarship: A Critical Introduction to Sociological Poetics.* Translated by Albert J. Wehrle. Baltimore: Johns Hopkins University Press, 1978.

Bailey, Randall C. "The Danger of Ignoring One's Own Cultural Bias in Interpreting the Text." Pages 66–90 in *The Postcolonial Bible.* Edited by R.S. Sugirtharajah. Sheffield: Sheffield Academic Press, 1998.

Bauckham, Richard. *The Jewish World Around the New Testament.* WUNT 1.233. Tübingen: Mohr Siebeck, 2008.

Bauer, Walter, F.W. Danker, W.F. Arndt, and F.W. Gingrich, eds. *A Greek-English Lexicon of the New Testament and Other Early Christian Literature.* 3rd edition. Chicago: University of Chicago, 2000.

Beetham, Christopher A. *Echoes of Scripture in the Letter of Paul to the Colossians.* Leiden: Brill, 2008.

Blomberg, Craig. *The Historical Reliability of John's Gospel: Issues and Commentary*. Downers Grove: InterVarsity, 2002.

Boer, Roland. *Marxist Criticism of the Bible*. London: T&T Clark International, 2003.

Bray, Gerald, ed. *Romans. Ancient Christian Commentary on Scripture. New Testament.* Vol. 6. Downers Grove: InterVarsity, 1998.

Brenton, Lancelot C.L. *The Septuagint with Apocrypha: Greek and English*. Peabody: Hendrickson, 1992.

Calvin, Jean. *The Epistles of Paul the Apostle to the Romans and to the Thessalonians*. Translated by Ross MacKenzie. Edited by David W. Torrance et al. Grand Rapids: Eerdmans, 1960.

Campbell, Douglas A. *The Deliverance of God: An Apocalyptic Rereading of Justification in Paul*. Grand Rapids: Eerdmans, 2009.

Casey, Maurice. "Where Wright Is Wrong: A Critical Review of N.T. Wright's Jesus and the Victory of God." *JSNT* 69 (1998): 95–103.

Chafer, Lewis S. *Dispensationalism*. Dallas: Dallas Seminary Press, 1936.

Charles, R.H. *The Assumption of Moses*. London: Adam and Charles Black, 1897.

_____. *The Apocrypha and Pseudepigrapha of the Old Testament in English*. 2 vols. Oxford: Clarendon Press, 1913.

Charlesworth, James H., ed. *The Old Testament Pseudepigrapha*. 2 vols. New York: Doubleday, 1983–1985.

Chrysostom, John. "Sixth Homily Against the Jews." Pages 147–75 in *Saint John Chrysostom: Discourses Against Judaizing Christians*. Edited by Paul W. Harkins and Hermigild Dressler. Washington, DC: Catholic University of America Press, 1999.

Cohen, Shaye J.D. *The Beginnings of Jewishness Boundaries, Varieties, Uncertainties.* Berkeley: University of California Press, 1999.

Collins, John C. *Jewish Wisdom in the Hellenistic Age.* Louisville: Westminster John Knox Press, 1997.

Collins, John J. *Daniel: A Commentary on the Book of Daniel.* Hermeneia. Edited by Frank Moore Cross. Minneapolis: Fortress Press, 1993.

_____. *The Scepter and the Star.* ABRL. New York: Doubleday, 1995.

_____. and P.W. Flint. *The Book of Daniel: Composition and Reception.* 2 Vols. Leiden: Brill, 2001–2002.

Colson F. H. *Philo VIII.* Cambridge: Harvard University Press, 1939.

Coogan, Michael D. ed., *The New Oxford Annotated Apocrypha: NRSV.* New York: Oxford University Press, 2010.

Cottrell, Jack. *Romans.* Vol. 2. CPNIV. Joplin: College Press, 1998.

Cranfield, C.E.B. *A Critical and Exegetical Commentary on the Epistle to the Romans.* 2 vols. ICC. Edinburgh: T&T Clark, 1975–1979.

Cross, Frank M. "Discovery of the Samaria Papyri." *BA* 26.4 (1963): 110–21.

Davies, Philip R. *1QM: The War Scroll from Qumran.* Rome: Biblical Institute, 1969.

Dever, William G. *What did the Biblical Writers Know and When did they Know It?: What Archaeology can tell us about the Reality of Ancient Israel.* Grand Rapids: Eerdmans, 2001.

Dimant, Devorah. *Parabiblical Texts Part 4: Pseudo-Prophetic Texts.* Oxford: Clarendon Press, 2001.

Driver, S. R. *An Introduction to the Literature of the Old Testament.* New York: Meridian Books, 1956.

Dube, Musa W. "Reading for Decolonization (John 4.1–42)," Pages 51–75 in *John and Postcolonialism: Travel, Space and Power*. Edited by Jeffrey Staley and Musa Dube. Sheffield: Sheffield Academic Press, 2005.

Dunn, James D.G. *Romans 1–8*. WBC 38A. Dallas: Word, 1988.

_____. *Romans 9–16*. WBC 38B. Dallas: Word, 1988.

_____. *The Theology of Paul the Apostle*. Grand Rapids: Eerdmans, 1998.

_____. *The New Perspective on Paul*. Grand Rapids: Eerdmans, 2008.

_____. *Jesus, Paul, and the Gospels*. Grand Rapids: Eerdmans, 2011.

Edersheim, Alfred. *The History of Israel and Judah: From the Reign of Ahab to the Decline of the Two Kingdoms*. New York: F.H. Revell, 1885.

Elliger, K. and W. Rudolph, eds. *Biblia Hebraica Stuttgartensia*. New edition. Stuttgart: Deutsche Bibelgesellschaft, 1977.

Fishbane, Michael A. *Biblical Interpretation in Ancient Israel*. Oxford: Clarendon Press, 1985.

_____. "Inner-Biblical Exegesis." Pages 33–48 in *Hebrew Bible, Old Testament: The History of Its Interpretation*. Edited by Magne Saebo. Vol. I. Göttingen: Vandenhoeck & Ruprecht, 1996.

Fitzmyer, Joseph A. *Romans: A New Translation with Introduction and Commentary*. AB 33. New York: Doubleday, 1993.

_____. *Tobit*. Berlin: Walter De Gruyter, 2003.

Gadd, C.J. "The Prism Inscriptions of Sargon." *Iraq* 16 (1954): 178–82.

Gentry, Peter J. and Stephen J. Wellum. *Kingdom through Covenant: A Biblical-Theological Understanding of the Covenants*. Wheaton: Crossway, 2012.

Goldstein, Jonathan. *II Maccabees*. AB 41A. New York: Doubleday, 1983.

González, Justo L. *A History of Christian Thought*. Vol. 2. Revised edition. Nashville: Abingdon Press, 1987.

Greimas A.J. and Joseph Courtés. *Semiotics and Language an Analytical Dictionary*. Translated by Larry Crist et al. Bloomington: Indiana University Press, 1982.

Halcomb, T. Michael W. *Entering the Fray: A Primer on New Testament Issues for the Church and the Academy*. Eugene: Wipe and Stock, 2012.

Harrington, Daniel J. *Paul on the Mystery of Israel*. Collegeville: Liturgical Press, 1992.

_____. *Invitation to the Apocrypha*. Grand Rapids: Eerdmans, 1999.

Hays, Richard B. *Echoes of Scripture in the Letters of Paul*. New Haven: Yale University Press, 1989.

_____. *The Faith of Jesus Christ: The Narrative Substructure of Galatians 3:1–4:11*. Grand Rapids: Eerdmans, 2002.

_____. *The Conversion of the Imagination: Paul as Interpreter of Israel's Scripture*. Grand Rapids: Eerdmans, 2005.

Hoekema, Anthony A. *The Bible and the Future*. Grand Rapids: Eerdmans, 1979.

Holland, Tom. *Romans: The Divine Marriage: A Biblical Theological Commentary*. Eugene: Wipf and Stock, 2011.

Hollander, John. *The Figure of Echo: A Mode of Allusion in Milton and After*. Berkeley: University of California Press, 1981.

Isasi-Diaz, Ada Maria. "By the Rivers of Babylon: Exile as a Way of Life" Pages 149–64 in *Reading from this Place*. Vol. 1. Edited by Fernando F. Segovia. Minneapolis: Fortress Press, 1995.

Jewett, R. "Romans as an Ambasadorial Letter" *Int* 36 (1982): 5–20.

_____. *Romans: A Commentary*. Hermeneia. Edited by Eldon J. Epp. Minneapolis: Fortress, 2007.

Johnson, Luke T. *Reading Romans*. New York: Crossroad, 1997.

Josephus. *Works of*. 10 vols. Loeb Classical Library. Translated by H. St. J. Thackeray et al. Cambridge: Harvard University Press, 1926–1965.

Käsemann, Ernst. *Commentary on Romans*. Translated and edited by Geoffrey W. Bromiley. Grand Rapids: Eerdmans, 1980.

Keener, Craig. *Romans*. NCCS. Cambridge: Lutterworth Press, 2009.

Keesmaat, Sylvia C. "Exodus and the Intertextual Transformation of Tradition in Romans 8:14-30." *JSNT* 54 (1994): 29–56.

_____. "Paul and his Story: Exodus and Tradition in Galatians." Pages 300–33 in *Early Christian Interpretation of the Scriptures of Israel: Investigations and Proposals*. Edited by C.A. Evans and J.A. Sanders. JSNTSup 148; SSEJC 5. Sheffield: Sheffield Academic Press, 1997.

Koch, Dietrich-Alex. *Die Schrift als Zeuge des Evangeliums: Untersuchungen zur Verwendung und zum Verständnis der Schrift bei Paulus*. BHT 69. Tübingen: Mohr-Siebeck, 1986.

Köstenberger Andreas J. *Encountering John: The Gospel in Historical, Literary, and Theological Perspective*. Grand Rapids: Baker Academic, 2013.

_____. and Richard D. Patterson. *Invitation to Biblical Interpretation: Exploring the Hermeneutical Triad of History, Literature, and Theology*. Grand Rapids: Kregel, 2011.

Kristeva, Julia. *Desire in Language: A Semiotic Approach to Literature and Art*. New York: Columbia University Press, 1980.

_____. *The Kristeva Reader*. Edited by Toril Moi. New York: Columbia University Press, 1986.

Kugel, James L. and Rowan A. Greer. *Early Biblical Interpretation*. Edited by Wayne A. Meeks. Philadelphia: Westminster, 1986.

Ladd, G.E. *The Meaning of the Millennium: Four Views*. Downers Grove, IL: InterVarsity, 1977.

Lampe, Peter. *Die Stadtrömischen Christen in den ersten beiden Jahrhunderten: Untersuchungen zur Sozialgeschichte*. WUNT 2.18. Tübingen: Mohr-Siebeck, 1987.

Law T.M. *When God Spoke Greek: The Septuagint and the Making of the Christian Bible*. Oxford: Oxford University Press, 2013.

Lee, Dorothy A. "John." Pages 709–34 in *The New Interpreter's Bible: One-Volume Commentary*. Edited by David L. Petersen and Beverly R. Gaventa. Nashville: Abingdon Press, 2010.

Lehrer, Steve. *New Covenant Theology: Questions Answered*. Tempe: IDS.org, 2006.

Lemche, Niels Peter. *The A to Z of Ancient Israel*. Lanham: Scarecrow Press, 2010.

Levenson, Jon. *Resurrection and the Restoration of Israel the Ultimate Victory of the God of Life*. New Haven: Yale University Press, 2006.

Levine, Amy-Jill and Marianne Blickenstaff, eds. *A Feminist Companion to Paul*. Cleveland: Pilgrim Press, 2004.

Liddell, H.G. and R. Scott. *A Greek-English Lexicon*. 9th revised edition. Oxford: Clarendon, 1940.

Lim, Timothy H. *Holy Scripture in the Qumran Commentaries and Pauline Letters*. Oxford: Clarendon, 1997.

Lipschitz, Oded. *Judah and the Judeans in the Persian Period*. Winona Lake: Eisenbrauns, 2006.

Luther, Martin. *On the Jews and Their Lies*. Translated by Martin H. Bertram. Philadelphia: Harpagon Press, 2014.

Marcus, Joel. *The Way of the Lord: Christological Exegesis of the Old Testament in the Gospel of Mark*. Louisville: Westminster John Knox, 1992.

Metzger, Bruce, ed. *A Textual Commentary on the Greek New Testament*. 2nd edition. Stuttgart: UBS, 1994.

Meyer, Ben F. *The Aims of Jesus*. London: SCM Press, 1979.

Moo, Douglas J. *The Epistle to the Romans*. NICNT. Grand Rapids: Eerdmans, 1996.

_____. *Romans*. NIVAC. Grand Rapids: Zondervan, 2000.

_____. "Paul's Universalizing Hermeneutic in Romans." *SBJT* 11.3 (2007): 62–90.

Nanos, Mark. *The Mystery of Romans: The Jewish Context of Paul's Letter*. Minneapolis: Fortress Press, 1996.

Newman, Carey C. *Jesus and the Restoration of Israel: A Critical Assessment of N.T. Wright's Jesus and the Victory of God*. Downers Grove: InterVarsity, 1999.

Nickelsburg, George W.E. *Jewish Literature Between the Bible and the Mishnah: A Historical and Literary Introduction*. Minneapolis: Fortress Press, 2005.

Piper, John. *The Future of Justification: A Response to N.T. Wright*. Wheaton: Crossway Books, 2007.

Pitre, Brant. *Jesus, the Tribulation, and the End of the Exile: Restoration Eschatology and the Origin of the Atonement*. WUNT 2.204. Tübingen: Mohr Siebeck, 2005.

Porter, Stanley E. and Christopher D. Stanley, eds. *As It Is Written: Studying Paul's Use of Scripture*. Atlanta: Society of Biblical Literature, 2008

Portier-Young, Anathea. "Languages of Identity and Obligation: Daniel as Bilingual Book." *VT* 60.1 (2010): 98–115.

Priest, J. "Testament of Moses: A New Translation and Introduction." Pages 919–34 in *The Old Testament*

Pseudepigrapha. Vol. 1. Edited by James H. Charlesworth. New York: Doubleday, 1983.

Pritchard, James B., ed. *Ancient Near Eastern Texts Relating to the Old Testament*. 3rd edition. Princeton, NJ: Princeton University, 1978.

Rahlfs, Alfred and Robert Hanhart, eds. *Septuaginta*. Stuttgart: Deutsche Bibelgesellschaft, 2007.

Rudolph, W. and K. Elliger. *Biblia Hebraica Stuttgartensia*. New edition. Stuttgart: Deutsche Bibelgesellschaft, 1977.

Sanders, E.P. *Paul and Palestinian Judaism: A Comparison of Patterns of Religion*. Philadelphia: Fortress Press, 1977.

_____. *Paul, the Law, and the Jewish People*. Philadelphia: Fortress, 1983.

_____. *Jesus and Judaism*. Philadelphia: Fortress Press, 1985.

Saussure, Ferdinand. *Course in General Linguistics*. Edited by Charles Bally and Albert Reidlinger. Translated by Wade Baskin. New York: Philosophical Library, 1959.

Schiffman, Lawrence H. *Reclaiming the Dead Sea Scrolls*. ABRL. New York: Doubleday, 1995.

Schreiner, Thomas R. *Romans*. BECNT. Grand Rapids: Baker Books, 1998.

_____. "Paul a Reformed Reading." Pages 19–47 in *Four Views on the Apostle Paul*. Edited by Michael F. Bird. Grand Rapids: Zondervan, 2012.

Schüssler, Elisabeth Fiorenza. *In Memory of Her: A Feminist Reconstruction of Christian Origins*. London: SCM, 1995.

Schweitzer, Albert. *The Mysticism of Paul the Apostle*. Translated by W. Montgomery. New York: Holt and Company, 1931.

_____. *The Quest of the Historical Jesus: A Critical Study of its Progress from Reimarus to Wrede*. Translated by W. Montgomery. Reprint. New York: Macmillan, 1968.

Sontag, Susan, ed. *A Barthes Reader*. New York: Hill and Wang, 1982.

Stanley, Christopher D. *Paul and the Language of Scripture: Citation Technique in the Pauline Epistles and Contemporary Literature*. SNTSMS 74. Cambridge: Cambridge University Press, 1992.

Staples, Jason A. "What do the Gentiles Have to Do with 'All Israel?' A Fresh Look at Romans 11:25–27." *JBL* 130.2 (2011): 371–90.

Stendahl, Krister. *Paul Among Jews and Gentiles and Other Essays*. Philadelphia: Fortress, 1976.

Tadmor, Hayim "The Aramaization of Assyria: Aspects of Western Impact." Pages 449–70 in *RAI* 25. Berlin: Dietrich Reimar, 1982.

Tanner, Paul. "The New Covenant and Paul's Quotation from Hosea in Romans 9:25–26." *BibSac* 162 (2005): 95–110.

Theissen, Gerd. *The Social Setting of Pauline Christianity: Essays on Corinth*. Translated by John H. Schütz. Edinburgh: T&T Clark, 1982.

Theodoret. "Interpretation of the Letter to the Romans." Pages 82.43–226 in *Patrologia graeca*. Edited by J.-P. Migne. 162 vols. Paris: Cramoisy, 1857–1886.

Tilling, Chris, ed. *Beyond Old and New Perspectives on Paul: Reflections on the Work of Douglas Campbell*. Eugene: Wipf and Stock, 2014.

Vermes, Geza, ed. *The Complete Dead Sea Scrolls in English*. Revised edition. London: Penguin Books, 2011.

Wagner, J. Ross. *Heralds of the Good News Isaiah and Paul in Concert in the Letter to the Romans*. Boston: Brill, 2003.

Wellhausen, Julius. *Prolegomena Zur Geschichte Israels*. 6 ausg. Berlin: Druck und Verlag von G. Reimer, 1905.

Williamson, H.G.M. *Ezra-Nehemiah*. WBC 16. Dallas: Word, 1985.
Witherington, Ben. *Paul's Letter to the Romans: A Socio-Rhetorical Commentary*. Grand Rapids: Eerdmans, 2004.
Wright, Jacob L. *David, King of Israel, and Caleb in Biblical Memory*. New York: Cambridge University Press, 2014.
Wright, N.T. *The Climax of the Covenant: Christ and the Law in Pauline Theology*. Edinburgh: T&T Clark, 1992.
_____. *The New Testament and the People of God*. Minneapolis: Fortress Press, 1992.
_____. *Jesus and the Victory of God*. Minneapolis: Fortress Press, 1996.
_____. *The Resurrection of the Son of God*. Minneapolis: Fortress Press, 2003.
_____. *Paul: In Fresh Perspective*. Minneapolis: Fortress Press, 2005.
_____. *Paul and the Faithfulness of God*. Minneapolis: Fortress Press, 2013.
Wright, Robert B. *The Psalms of Solomon: A Critical Edition of the Greek Text*. New York: T&T Clark, 2007.
Younger, K. Lawson. "The Deportations of the Israelites." *JBL* 117.2 (1998): 201–27.
Younger, K. Lawson and William W. Hallo, eds. *The Context of Scripture*. Vol. 2. Leiden: Brill, 2000.

Primary Sources

Greco-Roman
Ambrosiaster, *4-5*
John Chrysostom
  Adv. Jud., *11*
  Hom. Rom., *5*
Josephus
  Ant. 9.277–78, *61*
  Ant. 9.277–79, *63*
  Ant. 9.288–90, *65*
  Ant. 9.288–91, *71*
  Ant. 11.133, *110*
  Ant. 11.173, *36, 38, 110*
Philo, *108-109*
Theodoret, *5, 35*

OT Apocrypha
2 Macc 1:1–9, *100*
2 Macc 1:10–2:18, *100*
2 Macc 2:5, *100*
2 Macc 2:7, *100*
2 Macc 2:17, *101*
2 Macc 2:17–18, *101*
2 Macc 2:18, *101*
2 Macc 2:19–32, *100*
2 Macc 2:24–31, *55-56*
2 Macc 10:1–9, *101*
Sir 36:1–16, *95-97*
Sir 48:10, *95, 97, 106*
Sir 51:12, *95, 97*
Tob 1:1–3, *95*
Tob 1:9, *93*
Tob 1:10, *95*
Tob 1:10–12, *92*
Tob 2:11, *95*
Tob 3:4, *93*
Tob 4:12, *93*
Tob 4:12–13, *92*
Tob 5:9–14, *92*
Tob 8:1–3, *94*
Tob 11:14, *94*
Tob 12:1–5, *95*
Tob 13–14, *95*
Tob 13:3, *93*
Tob 13:5, *94*
Tob 14:4–7, *93-94*

OT Pseudepigrapha
4 Macc 17:22, *115*
Jub. 1:12–14, *97-98*
Jub. 1:22–25, *98-99*
Pss. Sol. 17:26, *16*
Pss. Sol. 17:26–32, *102*
Pss. Sol. 17:30, *16*
Pss. Sol. 17:31, *101*
T. Mos. 4:3, *104*

T. Mos. 4:5–9, *103-104*
T. Mos. 4:9, *104*

DEAD SEA SCROLLS
1QM, *48, 105-106*
1QM 1:1–3, *105*
1QM 1:2–3, *38*
4Q174, *48, 106*
4Q196–200, *92*
4Q200, *92*
4Q385, *48, 107-108*
4Q386, *48, 107-108*
4Q388, *48, 107-108*
4Q391, *107*

OLD TESTAMENT
Gen 1, *97*
Gen 15–17, *115*
Gen 18, *121*
Gen 18:10, *121-123, 126*
Gen 18:14, *121-123, 126*
Gen 21:12, *122*
Gen 32:28, *125*
Gen 48:16, *39, 125*
Gen 48:19, *39, 125-127*
Exod 9:16, *114*
Exod 11:9–10, *96*
Exod 12, *97*
Exod 15:6, *96*
Exod 19:5–6, 115
Exod 32:32, *113-114*
Exod 33:19, *114, 120, 121, 124*
Deut 4:34, *96*
Deut 29–31, *115*
Deut 30, *140*
Deut 31–34, *103*
Josh 8:30–35, *115*
2 Sam 23:5, *115*
1 Kgs 14:25–26, *58*
1 Kgs 21:1–15, *3*
2 Kgs 9–10, *3*
2 Kgs 15:19–20, *60*
2 Kgs 16:5–9, *60*
2 Kgs 17, *61, 72*
2 Kgs 17:6, *61, 67, 74*
2 Kgs 17:7–8, *72*
2 Kgs 17:24, *64*
2 Kgs 17:24–29, *71*
2 Kgs 17:25–26, *69*
2 Kgs 17:29–41, *68*
2 Kgs 17:33–34, *72*
2 Kgs 18:9–10, *61*
2 Kgs 18:11, 63 *67, 74*
2 Kgs 25:12, *63*
Ezra 4:1–2, *69, 72*
Ezra 4:3, *69*
Ezra 4:4, *68*
Ezra 9:1, *68*
Ezra 9:2, *68*
Ezra 10:10, *69, 72*
Ezra 10:18–44, *69, 72*
Neh 13:23–30, *69, 72*

Neh 13:24, *68-69*
Ps 44:22, *21*
Isa 1:9, *120*
Isa 2:2, *29*
Isa 2:2–4, *16*
Isa 10:5–19, *82, 131-132*
Isa 10:24, *82*
Isa 10:24–25, *82*
Isa 11, *84-85, 103, 127, 130*
Isa 11:1, *130-132*
Isa 11:10, *82-83, 131*
Isa 11:10–13, *81-82, 84*
Isa 11:11, *82*
Isa 11:13–14, *82, 132*
Isa 11:16, *82*
Isa 17, *129*
Isa 17:3–6, *129-130*
Isa 24–25, *132*
Isa 28–29, *135*
Isa 28:1–4, *135*
Isa 28:5, *136*
Isa 29:1–8, *135-136*
Isa 29:9–16, *136*
Isa 29:16, *120-121, 135*
Isa 40:3, *105*
Isa 45:9, *120-121, 135*
Isa 55:5, *115*
Isa 56:1–8, *143*
Isa 64:8, *120*
Isa 65:1, *21*
Jer 3:8, *84*

Jer 3:17–18, *84*
Jer 11, *129*
Jer 11:16–17, *129*
Jer 16:1–9, *2*
Jer 16:15, *91*
Jer 18:1–8, *120-121*
Jer 18:2–8, *134*
Jer 18:4, *134*
Jer 23, *103*
Jer 23:3, *91*
Jer 23:5–8, *85*
Jer 30:3–4, *84*
Jer 30:22, *84*
Jer 31, *87, 98*
Jer 31:1–22, *87, 127*
Jer 31:8, *84*
Jer 31:31–33, *99*
Jer 31:31–34, *86, 115*
Jer 31:34, *86, 91*
Ezek 4:9–17, *2*
Ezek 37, *28, 88-89*
Ezek 37–39, *89*
Ezek 37:1–14, *107-108*
Ezek 37:14, *88*
Ezek 37:15–28, *89*
Ezek 37:19–22, *28, 87-88*
Ezek 37:21–22, *88*
Ezek 37:23, *106*
Ezek 37:24, *88*
Ezek 37:26, *88*
Ezek 37:28, *89*
Ezek 39:21–29, *89*

Ezek 44:7, *143*
Dan 7–12, *89-90*
Dan 9:2, *90*
Dan 9:7, *90*
Dan 9:24, *91*
Dan 9:27, *91*
Dan 12:11–12, *89-90*
Hos 1, *98*
Hos 1:6, *3, 39, 141*
Hos 1:8, *3, 39*
Hos 1:9, *76, 84*
Hos 1:9–10, *1, 4-5, 30, 35, 45, 47-49, 111-112, 120-121, 146, 149-151*
Hos 1:10, *21, 138, 140-142*
Hos 1:10–11, *99*
Hos 1:11, *20, 28, 91*
Hos 2:19, *140*
Hos 2:23, *1, 4-5, 30, 35, 45, 47-49, 111-112, 120-121, 138, 140-141, 146, 149-151*
Hos 3:5, *92*
Hos 7:8, *39, 83*
Hos 8:8, *3, 27, 75, 134, 136-137*
Hos 9:17, *75*
Hos 14, *129*
Hos 14:4–7, *130, 132*
Joel 2:32, *21*

Mal 1:2–3, *121, 124*
Mal 2:10, *124*
Mal 2:12, *124*
Mal 2:15, *124*
Mal 3:16–21, *124*
Mal 4:5–6, *97*

NEW TESTAMENT
Acts 8:38, *17, 19, 23*
Rom 1:1–3, *52*
Rom 1:2, *117*
Rom 1:3, *118*
Rom 1:12, *122, 126*
Rom 1:16, *117*
Rom 1:16–17, *142*
Rom 2:9–10, *117*
Rom 2:25–3:31, *76, 116, 143*
Rom 2:28–29, *117, 121*
Rom 2:29, *143*
Rom 3:27–31, *143*
Rom 4:1–25, *123*
Rom 7:18, *122, 126*
Rom 8:28, *116*
Rom 8:29–30, *123*
Rom 9, *86, 112, 118-121, 123, 125, 133-134, 151*
Rom 9–11, *16, 52, 117*
Rom 9:1–23, *138*
Rom 9:3, *113-115*
Rom 9:4, *116-117, 119*

Rom 9:4–5, *113*
Rom 9:5, *118*
Rom 9:6, *117, 119, 128*
Rom 9:6–18, *118-124*
Rom 9:6–23, *121*
Rom 9:7–12, *120*
Rom 9:8, *118*
Rom 9:9, *121-123, 126*
Rom 9:11–23, *123*
Rom 9:13, *124, 142*
Rom 9:15, *114, 120, 124*
Rom 9:18, *121*
Rom 9:19–23, *133-138*
Rom 9:20, *135*
Rom 9:21, *134, 136-137*
Rom 9:21–22, *137*
Rom 9:22, *39, 136-137*
Rom 9:22–23, *114*
Rom 9:24, *117, 144*
Rom 9:24–26, *1, 4-5, 7, 10, 29, 33, 45, 47, 49, 51, 111-112, 138-147*
Rom 9:25–26, *4, 30, 77, 84, 112, 136, 139-141, 146*
Rom 9:25–29, *120*
Rom 9:26, *100, 128*
Rom 9:29, *121*

Rom 11, *112, 125*
Rom 11:1, *37, 117*
Rom 11:1–2, *128*
Rom 11:5, *121, 143*
Rom 11:11–12, *117*
Rom 11:17–24, *128-133*
Rom 11:24, *31*
Rom 11:25, *39, 121, 125-127*
Rom 11:25–27, *30*
Rom 11:27, *86-87, 91*
Rom 11:29, *117*
Rom 15, *82, 85*
Rom 15:6–7, *142*
Rom 15:8, *10, 117*
Rom 15:12, *82-84, 131*
Rom 15:27, *31*
1 Cor 15, *89, 91*
2 Cor 3, *86*
2 Cor 3:1–3, *87*
2 Cor 11:22, *37*
Gal 1:4, *3*
Gal 3, *86*
Gal 4, *86*
Gal 4:24, *115*
Eph 2, *86*
Phil 3:5, *37*
1 Pet 2:10, *8*

Modern Authors

Baden, J., *59*
Bakhtin, M. M., *40*
Bakhtin, M. M. & P. N. Medvedev, *40*
Bailey, R. C., *50*
Bauckham, R., *94*
Beetham, C. A., *24*
Blomberg, C., *55*
Boer, R., *50*
Bray, G., *4-5*
Calvin, J., *7, 123, 137*
Campbell, D. A., *25*
Casey, M., *79*
Chafer, L. S., *14*
Cohen, S. J. D., *35-36*
Collins, J. C., *95*
Collins, J. J., *90, 106*
Cottrell, J., *9-10, 35*
Cranfield, C. E. B., *7-9, 35, 83, 115, 126, 132, 136-137, 140-142*
Cross, F. M., *90*
Davies, P. R., *105*
Dever, W. G., *58-59*
Dimant, D., *107*
Dube, M. W., *50*
Dunn, J. D. G., *25, 83, 89, 113-117, 126, 132, 135-137, 140-142*
Edersheim, A., *67-68*
Evans, C. A., *80, 91, 94, 96, 100*
Finkelstein, I. & N. A. Silberman, *58*
Fishbane, M. A., *41-42*
Fitzmyer, J. A., *87, 92, 115, 123, 126, 132, 136-137, 142*
France, R. T., *3*
Gadd, C. J., *62*
Gentry, P. J. & S. J. Wellum, *18*
Goldstein, J., *100*
Gonzáles, J. L., *11*
Greimas, A. J. & J. Courtés, *40*
Harrington, D. J., *100*
Hays, R. B., *24, 41-46, 48, 112, 116, 119, 124, 126, 131-132, 134, 136, 140, 144-146, 151*
Hoekema, A. A., *14-15*
Holland, T., *89*
Hollander, J., *41*

Isasi-Diaz, A. M., *49-50*
Jewett, R., *87, 126, 132, 136, 142*
Johnson, L. T., *123*
Keener, C. S., *83*
Keesmaat, S. C., *46, 48*
Koch, D.-A., *34*
Köstenberger, A. J., *73*
Köstenberger, A. J. & R. D. Patterson, *54*
Kristeva, J., *40-41*
Kugel, J. L. & R. A. Greer, *53*
Ladd, G. E., *14-15, 17, 19*
Law, T. M., *34*
Lee, D. A., *6*
Lehrer, S., *22-23*
Lemche, N. P., *36-38*
Levenson, J., *89*
Levine, A.-J. & M. Blickenstaff, *49*
Lim, T. H., *34*
Lipschitz, O., *69*
Luther, M., *12-13*
Marcus, J., *105*
Meyer, B. F., *77*
Moi, T., *41*
Moo, D. J., *21-23, 37, 83, 115, 123, 126, 132, 136, 140, 142-144*
Nanos, M., *24*
Newman, C. C., *80*

Nickelsburg, G. W. E., *95, 97, 101, 103, 106*
Piper, J., *25*
Pitre, B., *27-29, 79-80, 89, 96, 102-103, 105-106*
Porter, S. E., *42*
Portier-Young, A., *90*
Priest, J., *104*
Sanders, E. P., *24, 26, 77, 79*
Saussure, F., *40*
Schiffman, L. H., *106*
Schreiner, T. R., *20-23, 83, 113-114, 126, 132, 135-137, 140, 142*
Schüssler, E. F., *49*
Schweitzer, A., *24, 77*
Sontag, S., *40, 45*
Stanley, C. D., *34*
Staples, J. A., *29-30, 36-38, 110, 126-127, 132, 136, 139-140*
Tadmor, H., *66-67*
Tanner, J. P., *139*
Theissen, G., *50*
Torrance, J. B., *18*
Wagner, J. R., *24, 34, 44, 81, 83, 113-114, 116, 123-124, 126, 132, 135-136, 141, 144-146*
Walvoord, J. F., *14*
Wellhausen, J., *2, 57*
Williamson, H. G. M., *69*

Witherington, B., *23*
Wright, J. L., *57-59, 74*
Wright, N. T., *3, 24-28, 35, 46-48, 77-80, 111, 123, 142-144, 146*

Wright, R. B., *102*
Younger, K. L., *60-65, 67-68, 75*

Subjects

Covenant Nomism, *25*
Covenant Theology, *18-23, 148*
   New Covenant Theology, *20-23*
Eschaton, *95*
   Inaugurated Eschatology, *79*
   Jewish restoration, *26, 79*
   Last Days, *3*
   Latter Days, *16, 92*
   Present Evil Age, *3*
   Resurrection of the Dead, *89, 107*
Exile
   Assyrian, *6, 9, 19, 21, 23, 27, 30, 79, 83, 104*
   Assyrian deportation and repopulation, *3, 61, 63-64, 70,*
   Babylonian, *19, 21, 23, 26-27, 29, 104-105, 108, 117*
   End of, *78, 81, 111, 150*
Federal Theology, *18*
Fullness of the Gentiles, *39, 125-128*
Hermeneutics

Authorial intent, *4, 16-17, 30, 49-52*
Deconstructionism, *50*
Feminist Criticism, *49*
Hermeneutic of reversal, *145-146*
Historical Criticism, *52*
Historical-Narrative, *10, 52*
Inner-biblical Exegesis, *41*
Intertextuality, *24, 41-42, 45*
Jewish hermeneutic, *4*
Liberation Theology, *50*
Marxist Criticism, *50*
Metalepsis, *41, 46, 124, 134, 139*
Narrative Criticism, *45, 52*
Narrative Intertextuality, *4, 45, 83*
Narrative Structualism, *45, 48*
Narrative Substructure, *45, 119, 151*
Paul's all-encompassing hermeneutic, *143*

Paul's arbitrary
    hermeneutic, *22*
Paul's hermeneutical
    coup, *144-45*
Postcolonial Criticism, *50*
Reader-response
    Criticism, *50*
Spiritualizing
    hermeneutic, *17*
Israel
    As ἐκκλησία, *17, 19*
    Election of, *26, 116, 118-119, 121-124, 127, 146*
    Ephraim, *28, 39, 81-82, 84, 87, 127-130, 132, 135, 138-140, 143*
    Ingathering of, *3, 10, 13, 16, 20, 29-31, 74, 81-82, 89, 95-97, 102, 105, 113, 127, 133, 139, 144, 147, 148*
    Realized promises, *16, 19-20, 79, 83, 133*
    Restoration of, *9, 25, 28, 59, 83, 87, 89-90, 94, 96, 100-101, 103, 106-107, 111, 147, 151*
    Southern Tribes, *10, 16, 35, 38, 104, 111, 135, 149-150*
    Northern Tribes, *1, 3-6, 8-10, 13-14, 16-17, 19, 21, 23, 27-31, 35-39, 60, 63-64, 67-69, 72-75, 79-80, 82-84, 87, 92, 94, 104-105, 110-113, 121, 125, 127-129, 132, 135, 137-144, 146-151*
New Perspective on Paul, *25,*
Premillennialism
    Dispensational, *14-18, 24, 139*
    Historic, *14-18*
    Parenthesis, *15*
Replacement Theology, *10, 13-15, 17-18, 21-24, 132, 148*
Samaritans, *6, 54, 68-70, 72-74*
Supersessionism, *10-14, 18*

www.ingramcontent.com/pod-product-compliance
Lightning Source LLC
Chambersburg PA
CBHW070046230426
43661CB00005B/786